ENJOY BEGINNING BRIDGE BY A RECENT BEGINNER

ENJOY LEARNING BEGINNING BRIDGE

BY A RECENT BEGINNER

A How-to-Play-Bridge Book for Beginners & Card Players long Overdue for a Tune-up

Beginning Bridge involves Learning Fundamentals and a Second Language---"Bridge Speak"

Too Often, Beginning Bridge Books Convert Bridge Beginners into Canasta Players

Being Fluent in Bridge makes you a more Interesting and Self-Confident Individual

Unlike too many Card Games, Bridge is not a Fad; it's been around for over 400 Years

Investing your Time in Learning Bridge is not an Investment in a Diminishing Asset

Bridge's Future Lies with its Beginners---Those Who Read and Absorb what they Read

Speed Reading is the friend of Comic Strip Readers, not Beginning Bridge Players

AuthorHouse™
1663 Liberty Drive
Bloomington, IN 47403
www.authorhouse.com
Phone: 1-800-839-8640

Copyright © The Recent Beginner. All rights reserved.

No part of this book may be reproduced, stored in a retrieval system, or transmitted by any means without the written permission of the author.

First published by AuthorHouse 5/6/2010

ISBN: 978-1-4490-0861-1 (sc)
ISBN: 978-1-4490-0948-9 (e)

Library of Congress Control Number: 2009909070

Printed in the United States of America
Bloomington, Indiana

This book is printed on acid-free paper.

DEDICATION

This book is dedicated to the former City College of New York, School of Business and Civic Administration. In its day, it was known as "The Poor Man's Harvard," graduating what became some of the best public accountants and entrepreneurs in the country. It has since been renamed the Baruch College. It continues, to this day, as a commuter school, providing a first rate education to a diversity of first rate students. I was privileged to attend this school and am as proud of it today as I was then. But my greatest debt to this outstanding institution is that it introduced me to the most beautiful girl in the world, Felice Rochman Giordano, my wife of over 50 years, mother and mother-in-law to the parents who produced the best 11 grandchildren on this planet: Tony, Tracy, Peter, James, Sarah, John, Michael, Sam, Carley, Christen and Jack Robert. May all their bids be made!

CONTENTS

Chapter 1: Introduction to Beginning Bridge — 11
    What Makes Bridge so Special?

Chapter 2: Mechanics of Bridge — 15
    The Auction, the Play of the Tricks and the Scoring
    The Preliminaries, Guidelines
    The Proprieties, Bridge Etiquette and Customs
    Mechanics of Cards, Distributions, Hand Shapes
    Bridge Diagramming
    Bridge Conversations between New Partners

Chapter 3: Point-Count Systems, Counting Sure Winners and Hand Valuations — 19
    "How High and Where" the Bidding Goes
    Determining Trick-Taking Potential: Initial and Final Point-Counts
    Declarer Values his Hand
    Responder Revalues as Likely Dummy
    The Perfect Bridge Hand
    Illustrations:
        Matrix: Counting Sure Winners Combined and Single Hands — 21
        Figure # 1 Beginner's Bidding Ladder — 23
        Quiz # 1: Hand Valuations — 24

Chapter 4: First Seat Determines the Where" Part of the Opening Bid — 27
    Where You Sit is What You are Called
    The Priorities When Choosing of the "Where" Part of the Opening Bid
    Opening Bids at the One-Level
    The Hazards of Playing in Notrump
    Opening Bids in a Major
    Part-Score in a Minor is Better than No-score in a Minor
    Strategy and Tactics for Opening Bids
    The Controversial Rule of Twenty for Opening Suit Bids
    Hand Shapes versus Point-Counts
    Preemptive Opening Suit Bids at Levels 2-4
    The Rule of Two and Three and Sacrifice Bids
    Brief Tutorial on Rubber Scoring and Tradeoff Analyses
    The Artificial, Strong 2-Club Opening Bid
    The 2-Notrump Opening Bid.
    Illustrations
        Matrix: Choosing between Opening Bids in Notrump and in a Suit — 35
        Quiz #2: Varieties of Opening Bids — 36

Chapter 5: Mechanics of the Bidding Process — 39
    The Proprieties of the Bidding Process
    The Key to the Bidding Conversation
    Competitive versus Non-Competitive Auctions
    The "Bill of Rights" of the Bidding Process
    The Beginners Bidding Agreement
    SCRIPT: Two New Partners and their Bidding Agreement Conversation — 41

Chapter 6: Second Seat Reacts to the Enemy's Opening Bid   **43**
        The Suit Overcall Dances to the Opening Suit's Tune
        Simple Suit Overcalls at Levels 1 & 2
        When the Fourth Seat Overcalls
        Why Overcall an Opening Bid
        The Trap Pass: When to Not Overcall an Opening Bid
        Preemptive Overcalls
        Notrump Overcalls: 1-Level Yes; 2-Level, Never
        The Double for Takeout and its Acceptable Shapes
        Bidding a Double to Keep the Auction Alive
        Challenging Notrump Opening Bids with Suit Overcalls
        Illustrations
             Matrix: Suit and Notrump Overcalls   **47**
             Quiz # 3: Second Seat Responds to Opening Bids   **48**

Chapter 7: Third Seat Responds to a Wide Variety of Opening Bids   **53**
        The Third Seat's Role and Priorities
        The three Notrump Balanced Shapes: Identifying 8-card Fits
        The Trick-Taking Magic of the 8-Card Golden Fit
        The Law of Total Tricks and its Limits
        Responding to Notrump Openings
        Transfer Bidding (the Jacoby)
        The Stayman Bidding Conversation
        Responding to Major Suit Openings with Support and without Support
        Responding in Notrump
        Responding in Minor Suits: Why they are the Last Choice
        Responding with a Jump Shift to a Minor Suit Opening
        Responding to Preemptive Openings
        The Negative Double
        No Bidding Beyond 3-Notrump in Beginning Bridge
        Responding to the Strong 2-Club Artificial Opening Bid
        Responding after Partner Opens in 7-Notrump
        Illustrations:
             Figure # 2: Probability Table of Card Divides   **67**
             Quiz # 4: Third Seat Responds to a Variety of Opening Bids   **68**

Chapter 8: Fourth Seat Advances Overcalls and Takeout Doubles   **75**
        Advancing 1-level Overcalls with 3-Card Support and Weakness
        Understanding the Law of Total Tricks
        Advancer's Priorities
        Advancing the Overcall
            In a Cuebid
            Without a Cuebid
        When Support for Major Suit Overcall Unavailable:
            Advance other Major as a New Suit
            Advance in 1-Notrump
            Advance in a New Minor Suit
        Advancing the 1-Notrump Overcall:
            With a Transfer Bid or Stayman
            In 2-Notrump
        Advancing Preemptive Overcalls

        Advancing the Double
            In a Suit
            In Notrump
            In a Cuebid
        When the Advancer Passes a Takeout Double: The "Ticking Time Bomb"
        Fourth Seat Balances
        Illustrations:
            Quiz # 5: Advancing Overcalls and Takeout Doubles   **82**

Chapter 9: Opening Lead Cards and the Strategy of Defense   **87**

        Select the Opening Suit before Selecting the Opening Lead Card
        Mechanics of Suits, Sequences and Cards
        The Carding Decision: Selecting the Opening Lead Suit and then the Card
        The Rule of Eleven and Fourth Best
        Illustrations:
        Matrix: Convention Card Opening Leads   **90**
            Quiz # 6: Opening Leads   **91**

Chapter 10: The End Game: Planning of the Play and the Play of the Tricks   **93**

        Declarer Play
        Mechanics of the Play of the Tricks
        Declarer's Tally
        Developing Extra Needed Tricks
        Trump Suit Management
        Drawing Trumps from the Enemy
        Keeping Mental Track of the Trumps
        Trumping Losers in the Dummy
        Discarding Sure Losers
        Developing Winners through Promotion and Length
        Developing Extra Tricks through Finesse
        Teaching Virtual Bridge versus Teaching Real Bridge
        Data Point Events
        Getting from the Deal to the End Game:
        Planning the Play of the Trick
        Strategy of the Play of the Tricks
        Handling of the Tricks
        Planning of the Play Scenarios
            # 1 Lady Luck and Finesse   **103**
            # 2 Flirting with the Law of Total Tricks   **109**
            # 3 Stayman   **115**

        Looking Beyond Beginning Bridge:
            Slam Bidding
            The Rarest Perfect Bridge Hand

Chapter 11: Scoring Formats, Vulnerabilities and Tradeoffs   **123**

        Rubber Scoring Format Scoring Events
        Partnerships are Vulnerable and Contracts are Doubled
        Guidance for Bidding a Penalty Double
        Mechanics of the Score Card
        Scoring a 10 Deal Sample Rubber to Final Settlement

Illustrations:
    Matrix: Trick-Score Point Table
                   Undertrick Penalty Table
                   Overtrick Bonus Table
                   Bonus Points
                   Rubber Bonus Point Table
                   Insult Bonus
                   Game Bid Table
    Figure # 3: Score Card for a Sample 10 Deal Rubber   **133**
    Figure # 4: Scoring in a Duplicate Bridge Scoring Format   **134**
          Translating the Duplicate Scoring Table

Chapter 12: The End of Beginning Bridge   137

    The Climax: The End of Beginning Bridge and the Beginning of Intermediate
    Some Bridge Skills beyond Beginning Bridge
        Convention Cards
        Duplicate Contract Bridge
        Competitive Auctions
        Slam Bidding
        Two-Over-One Game Force
        Double for Penalty
        Signaling
        Balancing
        Redouble
    Sources for Skills beyond Beginning Bridge   **139**

Acknowledgements   9

Foreword   10

Bibliography   140

Glossary of Bridge Terms/Index   141

ACKNOWLEDGEMENTS

Development of this book's basic format involved an extensive search within the limited body of beginning bridge literature dedicated to the beginner. While a listing of all the books involved would not be particularly helpful, the resources listed in the Bibliography were considered especially important to the development of this book. Audrey Grant's significant contribution in *Bridge Basics 1 and Bridge Basics 2*, especially the orderly manner with which bridge guidelines were presented, was an inspiration in the launch of this book. Richard Pavlicek's pioneering efforts in providing budding bridge authors with bridge-writing style guidance was invaluable. In Pavlicek's *Bridge Writing Style Guide,* his work on bridge diagrams in general and the play diagrams in particular, is a breakthrough. The clarity of prose and the illuminated graphics in Peter Arnold's *Basic Bridge* was exceptional. His section on scoring, on a deal-by-deal basis is a landmark approach to the acquisition of this important and oft-neglected bridge skill. The comprehensive and authoritative guidance provided in Henry's *Official Encyclopedia of Bridge* and Brown's *Bridge Players' Dictionary* greatly simplified the task of translating essential "Bridge Speak" terms into "beginning bridge English." William Root's award winning book, *How to Play a Bridge Hand,* was of invaluable assistance to this "recent beginner," especially in the intricacies of handling suit combinations. Larry Cohen's "Law of Total Tricks" is a mainstay of this book and seamlessly bridges the gap between point-counts and counts of Sure Winners. Brent Manley's *The Tao of Bridge* and his 200 principles is the perfect highway for the Beginner to arrive at "Intermediate Land" and beyond.

In addition to published sources, I have been humbled by Martin Zucker's personal dedication of his time and talent to this project. An awesome bridge scholar, he is recognized as a Life Master, the highest basic category into which the ACBL ranks a player; an ACBL Certified Director; an ACBL Certified Teacher; a Past President of the North Jersey Bridge Association of the ACBL; Teacher and Bridge Director on numerous cruises; and, host of the BallenIsles C.C. televised Channel 63 daily show: *Bridge Tips.* This book would not have been credible without the bridge guidance provided by Martin Zucker. His guidance is always swift, unhesitating, invariably on-target and delivered with a much appreciated soft touch.

Whatever errors remain is solely the responsibility of this "Recent Beginner."

Andrew Giordano

FOREWORD

It was almost inevitable that Andy Giordano, as a sitting member of Dale Carnegie's Board of Directors, would write a "How To" book, one of the major niches of the publishing world. Over 70 years ago, Dale Carnegie wrote one of the world's most successful "how to" books, *"How to Win Friends and Influence People."* Andy's book, "How to" Enjoy Beginning Bridge is sure to be an important member of that publishing genre.

As Dale Carnegie's works have evolved into a major force in modern management practices, Bridge has also evolved into "modern bridge;" and, is now an even much more pleasant way in which to invest your time. Earning the skills of bridge is a timeless badge of honor and stimulating mental challenge, worthy of the best and the brightest.

This book will be a treat for those who are just learning to play bridge. It is straightforward. It is clear. It is comprehensive. While aimed at the beginner, it offers important tips for the inevitable next step: Intermediate Bridge.

Relax. Be patient. Enjoy! As the Admiral says: You are in for a great sail and he is providing the "fair winds and the following seas."

Peter Handal
Chairman, CEO
Dale Carnegie and Associates
New York City

CHAPTER 1

DO I REALLY WANT TO LEARN HOW TO PLAY BRIDGE?

Before the beginner undertakes this journey, it should be understood that, in bridge, as in life, there is no free lunch. Learning the fundamentals of bridge requires an investment of both your time and your full attention. Presumably, you are literate and enjoy mentally stimulating challenges; otherwise, you would not be reading this book. If that assumption is valid, bridge may be the skill set in which you want to invest some of your time. Perhaps you have tried to learn bridge at an earlier time in your life but found it was too complicated and simply abandoned the effort. You also may have played social bridge for some time and now feel your bridge education needs to be updated. In either case, *Enjoy Beginning Bridge* is the book you are looking for. It is dedicated to providing you with the skills to become "bridge literate" in a logical and entertaining way. Having recently gone through the experience---the hard way---by hitting every bump in the road, I am committed to repaving the road and making it a much smoother ride.

The following are a series of questions you may be asking yourself before you start this trip with this book as your guide. Hopefully, these answers will help you decide if both bridge and this book are for you.

WHAT MAKES BRIDGE SO SPECIAL?

The play of Bridge presents never-ending intellectual challenges. As your bridge prowess develops, so do your powers of concentration, memory and retention. Also, since it takes four players, bridge is an entertaining and social way to enhance those skills. Being "fluent" in bridge makes you a more interesting and self-confident person. Finally, you will not be investing your time in a diminishing asset. Unlike many other card games, bridge is not a fad. It is for good reason that bridge, in one form or another, has been around for almost 400 years. You will be learning a valuable and enduring skill.

WHY WOULD I WANT TO LEARN BRIDGE FROM A RECENT BEGINNER?

Most "how-to" books---including those on bridge are written by genuine experts. The problem is that, over time, experts forget what it was like to be a beginner and tend to write in "bridge shorthand," assuming that all readers are at the same level of development. While it may sound counterintuitive, I am convinced that there is a role for a "Recent Beginner" in teaching beginning bridge, especially a literate one, with a penchant for and experience in teaching. Be assured that I know the limitations of a beginner and, without requesting reciprocity, will refrain from providing guidance that requires the depth of experience that only experts can provide.

HOW WILL THIS BOOK BE DIFFERENT FROM OTHER BEGINNING BRIDGE BOOKS?

While it is natural for beginners to try to memorize guidelines the better approach is to understand the *why* of the guidance. When there is an opportunity to explain the logic and rationale behind a guideline, we will do so. We call these explanations, "Bridge-Logic."

Advanced bridge players have a "clubby" way of communicating. It is truly another language. We call those clubby phrases "Bridge-Speak." For example, when advanced players finally "make" a game they become "vulnerable." We will always be on the look-out for "Bridge-Speak" impediments to learning and will make the necessary translations for you. Learning bridge without those translations is like watching a foreign film without sub-titles!

The first time a new bridge term is introduced, it will be defined and displayed in **BOLD,** with all letters capitalized. For example, the first time you see the term "trick," it will appear as follows: "**TRICK,** four cards played in rotation with winner playing the best card." Obviously, in the early chapters of Enjoy Beginning Bridge, there will be more new bridge terms than you will see in the later chapters.

The book's format is specifically designed for a beginner, with three separate sections within each major chapter: a narrative which explains the specific bridge skill that is introduced; a matrix that summarizes the guidelines discussed in the narrative; and, a series of quizzes which include solutions and a "lessons learned" section that transcends the specific problem.

Finally, *Beginning Bridge* devotes a separate chapter to each of the four different bridge roles a player must be prepared to assume: as the First Seat, when he opens the bidding; as the Second Seat when he challenges the opening bid made by his opponent; as the Third Seat when he responds to the opening bid made by his partner in the First Seat; and, as the Fourth Seat when he **ADVANCES**, "Bridge-Speak" for responding to the challenges made by his partner in the Second Seat.

WHAT KIND OF BRIDGE IS TAUGHT IN *BEGINNING BRIDGE*?

Over the years, **CONTRACT SOCIAL BRIDGE,** also known as **CONTRACT BRIDGE** has retained its popularity because it is played in a *social setting* for moderate or no stakes where partnerships compete against each other. Contract bridge is frequently and inaccurately referred to as **RUBBER BRIDGE.** In fact, the **RUBBER,** a best two out of three match, is the scoring format used when playing Contract Bridge. Since beginners tend to first learn bridge in an informal setting, *Beginning Bridge* is devoted exclusively to the play of Contract Social Bridge using the Rubber Scoring Format, the details of which are fully discussed in Chapter 11, Scoring Formats.

Another popular form of bridge is **CONTRACT DUPLICATE BRIDGE,** more frequently known as **DUPLICATE;** and, played in *organized settings* such as tournaments. In Duplicate, the deal is pre-determined by the tournament's directors aided by a computer. The same exact deal is played by many different partnerships, known as **PAIRS** at the same time. The winning Pair is the team that outperforms all the other teams playing the same deal. Usually, Intermediate and Advanced players prefer duplicate bridge because it eliminates "the luck of the deal." While the bidding and the playing of the tricks are basically the same in both bridge forms, the different scoring format requires certain strategies to be different than what would be used in a Rubber Scoring format. In Chapter 11: Scoring Formats, Vulnerabilities and Tradeoffs, both scoring formats are discussed in some depth. As a beginner, be assured that you will need the skills discussed in *Enjoy Beginning Bridge before* you can contemplate playing in duplicate.

HOW LONG TO BECOME A SOCIALLY ACCEPTABLE BEGINNING BRIDGE PLAYER?

The answer, of course, depends on the amount of time you are willing to invest and how you invest that time. If you are a literate person, I would think your preference would be a book over group lessons. In the latter situation, the range of beginning bridge skills can be as wide as there are students; and, large classes can become a "Tower of Babel" with each student communicating in his own level of "Bridge-Speak." With a book you can learn bridge at your own pace, one usually very different from your classmates.

Note that I have added "socially acceptable" to the list of attributes required of a beginner. While I am not advocating a Dale Carnegie persona at the bridge table, after all this is a competitive sport, I am suggesting that there is a need to play at a tempo that is not distractingly slow. When a more advanced player agrees to play with a beginner, his patience should not be challenged by slow play. As in tennis, "playing up" is a wonderful way to learn bridge.

DO I NEED TO HAVE A HIGH IQ WITH GOOD MATHEMATICAL SKILLS?

While bridge is not for dummies, at least not my definition of a dummy, you do not need to be a member of MENSA to enjoy and excel in the game. A literate person, with good reading skills, and a willingness to invest a reasonable amount of time and energy should be all that is needed. As for mathematics, there is no bridge strategy I have encountered that requires anything more complex than simple arithmetic. The most important number in bridge is 13, for the number of cards in your hand and the number of tricks played in every deal. Every calculation starts from the number 13.

DO I NEED TO HAVE A GOOD MEMORY?

While learning any skill requires familiarizing oneself with important guidelines, nothing remotely approaching a photographic memory is required. We all think we need a better memory than the one we have. In fact, one of the reasons for bridge's popularity is that it exercises your powers of concentration, which, in turn, enhances your retention skills. There are two points to remember about memory: it gets better with mental exercise; and, you cannot remember everything!

DO I NEED TO BE A GAMBLER IN ORDER TO ENJOY BRIDGE?

First of all, let's exclude penny-a-point stakes from the definition of gambling! For me, the stimulation comes from the mental exercise, not from gambling. Having said that, I find that penny ante bridge adds spice to the game and more importantly, dampens irrational exuberance during the auction.

HOW WIL I KNOW WHEN I AM NO LONGER A BRIDGE BEGINNER

The short answer is when you have absorbed the skills introduced in *Beginning Bridge* .The longer answer is when you start to be frustrated by the inability of your skills to win more tricks than you are now winning. A sure clue is when you start to notice that you are leaving points on the table because your bidding skills did not permit you to fully achieve the trick-taking potential of your hand. To help you make the transition to the next level of bridge, Chapter 12: The Climax lists those bridge skills that are considered to be beyond beginning bridge level.

So, fair winds and following seas, you are in for a great sail!

CHAPTER 2

THE MECHANICS OF BRIDGE

Bridge is a series of three major transactions, starting with the **AUCTION** which gives the side that **BID** the highest numbers of tricks the right to **DEFINE THE CONTRACT:** to decide whether the game will be played in trumps or in Notrump. As in business, winning a contract comes with a reward when it is **FULFILLED** (when the side makes all the tricks it bid) and a **PENALTY,** a score arising from the failure of a contract (make fewer tricks than bid). For example, if play in a 4-level contract requiring 10 tricks, yields only 9 tricks, the contract is **SET**, defeated and the defense is awarded all the penalty points incurred by the offense, who scores zero points. The losing side, with 10 tricks bid and 9 tricks made, is said to **GO DOWN** one trick.

The second major transaction is the **PLAY OF THE TRICKS,** made up of 13 tricks from the opening lead card to the 52nd card played; determines whether the contract is fulfilled. Since there are 13 tricks in the play of the hand, there can be no tie. Each trick involves the play of four cards. If a contract promises 10 tricks, 6 tricks over book, defense only needs 4 tricks in order to defeat the contract.

The third and last major bridge transaction is the **SCORING**, which tallies up the points earned in a deal. If less than the 100 points required for game are scored, more deals are required until a side achieves at least 100 points, the minimum points needed to win one game. In a Rubber Scoring Format, the first side to win two out of three games wins the Rubber and scores a **RUBBER BONUS**. No points are awarded when the sides win games in a **RUBBER**; When a Rubber is won 2-0 the Rubber Bonus is significantly higher than when the Rubber is won 2-1.

BRIDGE GUIDELINES VERSUS THE LAWS OF CONTRACT BRIDGE

GUIDELINES are not to be confused with the **LAWS OF CONTRACT BRIDGE;** guidelines are suggestions for successfully executing bridge transactions such as making the contract, when on **OFFENSE**; or, defeating a contract, when on **DEFENSE**. While it may be good bridge strategy to occasionally ignore a guideline, beginners should always be on the lookout for when that is appropriate. However, it is never good strategy to break the Law. As the beginner will note, the words "never" and "always" are rarely used in bridge literature.

Guidelines are developed in many ways, the most usual of which is by observing successful strategies. In *Enjoy Beginning Bridge,* guidance provided was mainly derived from the sources listed in the Bibliography. Bridge guidance has two main characteristics: it is a suggestion, not a rule since there can be more than one way to successfully execute a transaction; and, since guidance is not static, it will change over time as more winning strategies are developed. Better bridge players are noted for their devotion to the game and their willingness to always learn about the "latest and greatest" guidance.

On the other hand, the Laws of Contract Bridge are not guidelines that may or may not be followed. The 81 Laws are not debatable. When a law is "broken," in formal play, **PENALTY POINTS** are imposed against the offender. For example, when a player fails to follow suit, when able to do so and either member of the offending side plays to the next trick, the Law has been broken; in this case the misdemeanor is a **REVOKE** and penalties, as specified by the Laws, apply.

BIDDING AGREEMENT CONVERSATIONS BETWEEN NEW PARTNERS

So that misunderstandings do not arise between beginners during the bidding process, a **BIDDING AGREEMENT DISCUSSION** is held, especially between new partners, to ensure that both partners are following the same guidance and what certain bids mean when used in an Auction. In Chapter 5: The Mechanics of the Bidding Process, a scripted Bidding Agreement Conversation is provided to describe how two beginning bridge players who have never played together should go about describing their level of play.

THE MECHANICS OF BRIDGE CARDS

Before there can be an auction or the playing of the tricks, two decks are used: one for the play of the tricks; and one to maintain the tempo between deals. A standard deck of cards, *one without a Joker*, has many characteristics: four Suits, distinguished by color: black for Spades and Clubs, and red for Hearts and Diamonds. Within each of the four suits, there are 13 cards divided into two categories of rank: major suits, consisting of Spades and Hearts; and, minor suits, consisting of Diamonds and Clubs. Any major suit card outranks any minor suit card while Diamonds outrank Clubs.

When the side that wins an auction decides to not name a trump suit, the game is played in **NOTRUMP**, a virtual suit for bidding and ranking purposes. In bidding, it is a fundamental Law that each succeeding bid must outrank the preceding bid. For bidding purposes, Notrump outranks all the suits. The four suits and Notrump are collectively known as **STRAINS**, ranked in descending order: Notrump, Spades, Hearts, Diamonds and Clubs.

Suit rankings break ties when two competing bids, in different suits, bid the same number of tricks. For example, when a bid of 1-heart is followed by an opponent's bid of 1-spade, the Spade bid outranks Hearts. In addition to suit rankings, individual cards also have ranks: the highest are the four **HIGH CARDS**, AKQJ, ranking in that order and also known as **FACE CARDS**. The High Cards are followed by nine **SPOT** cards, 10 98765432, for a total of 13 cards in each **HAND**. The Ace, King, Queen, Jack and spot 10 are known as **HONOR CARDS** and are especially important when you are valuing a suit's **STRENGTH**, its trick-taking potential.

THE MECHANICS OF GETTING THE GAME STARTED, THE PRELIMINARIES

Before a game of contract bridge can get started, decisions, known as the **PRELIMINARIES** need to be made. For example: which of the four players becomes the **DEALER**, the one who distributes the cards to the players; which player wins the opportunity to make the first call; how is the randomness of the cards ensured; what is the most efficient way of sorting the 13 cards dealt to each player; what is the protocol for dealing the cards; and, how and when are the cards picked up after the deal is completed?

The answers to these fundamental questions are included in the draw, shuffle, cut. deal and sort bridge acts. The draw begins when the four players select one card each from a deck, spread out and face-down. The two highest cards form one partnership and the next two are on the other side. Following the draw is the shuffle, the event that ensures the random distribution of the cards. This is followed by the cut, performed by two opposing players who split the deck to further ensure randomness. The cut always takes place before the cards are distributed by the dealer. A deck is considered **MADE** when properly shuffled and cut. A made deck is moved to the right of the player who will be the next dealer.

All these bridge acts culminate in the **DEAL**, the distribution of 52 cards, one-by-one and face-down and in a clockwise rotation. If the deal has been made properly, the dealer will get the last card. While the deal is in progress, the dealer's partner shuffles the second deck and passes it to his right. At the end of the deal, each of the four players will have 13 cards.

Prior to the sort, the players should count their cards while they are still face-down to ensure that there has been no **MISDEAL,** when one player has one card more or less than the allotted 13 cards. Should that happen, the deck is considered "deficient" and the remedy is to have the same dealer **REDEAL** the hand. After ensuring that there has been no misdeal, the players sort their hands, usually by suit and rank within each suit and begin the play of the tricks.

MECHANICS OF THE PROPTIETIES: BRIDGE ETTIQUETE, PROTOCOLS AND CUSTOMS

The Laws of Contract Bridge are in two parts: the first part is *procedural*, dictating the rules of play: and, the second part, **PROPRIETIES** meticulously prescribe the *behavior* of the players.

For example, there should be no conversation during the deal; players should not watch the cards as they are being dealt; players should not pick up their hands until all the cards have been distributed; and, players should sort their suits without expressing pleasure or displeasure with the cards dealt.

THE MECHANICS OF DISTRIBUTION

After the deal's 52 cards are distributed, each player holds 13 cards. Since distribution of the suits is random, a hand can vary from one extreme with 13 cards all in one suit and three void suits to the most common distribution, a 4-4-3-2 shape with cards in all four suits. The only constant in all this randomness is that the sum of the cards in a single Hand cannot exceed 13. A 4-card or longer suit is considered a **LONG SUIT**; and, is said to have **LENGTH,** a feature that enhances a suit's trick-taking potential, especially when a game is played in notrump. A suit of 2 or fewer cards is considered a **SHORT SUIT,** a feature known as **SHORTNESS** that also enhances trick-taking potential. When a short suit becomes void, a trump suit may be used to win a trick led by the other side in the suit that is now void. Shortness for point-count purposes exists in a suit only when it contains a void, a doubleton, or a singleton.

THE MECHANICS OF HAND SHAPES

An individual hand of 13 cards is described by its **SHAPE,** numbers of cards held in each suit. A description of a Hand's shape may be "4-4-3-2," shorthand for a shape that has two 4-card suits, one 3-card suit and one 2-card suit. What this method of description does not indicate is *which* of the suits are the 4-card suits, 3-card suits or 2-card suits. There are 39 possible hand shapes, of which only three are defined as **BALANCED HANDS**, the 4-3-3-3, the most perfectly balanced shape, known as such since it has no shortness; the 4-4-3-2 and the 5-3-3-2 shapes, both of which have shortness (doubletons). All 36 of the other possible hand shapes are unbalanced hands.

When you take into account the four different suits within the 39 possible hand shapes, the number of possible hands totals over 635 trillion. This virtually infinite variety of different hands is what makes the challenge of bridge never-ending. It also makes it impossible to memorize a strategy for each one of the possible Hands you might encounter. *Finally, there are instances when a Hand's shape may be a more important indicator of a hand's trick-taking potential than its point-count strength.* That phenomenon is discussed more fully in Chapter 4: First Seat Determines the "How High and Where" parts of the opening bid..

THE FOLLOW-THE-SUIT LED LAW

While the leader of a trick may lead with any card he has in his hand, the Law requires that the other three players, if they have any card of the suit led, must follow with a card from that suit. *If a player has more than one card of the suit led, he is not required to play the higher one.* If a player does not have a card of the suit led, he can **DISCARD;** use a card which is not of the suit led and not of the trump suit. Stated another way, in the latter example, a trump card need not be played. After all four players follow suit, discard or use a trump, the trick is won by the highest card in the suit led or by the trump card.

THE MECHANICS OF BRIDGE DIAGRAMMING

The graphic portrayal of bridge transactions, as opposed to narration, is known as diagramming. The problem with narratives is that they are extremely cumbersome and subject to misinterpretation. As a result, it was inevitable that bridge authors would devise a method for portraying bridge hands graphically. **DIAGRAMMING** is an efficient alternative to a narrative. There are three types of bridge diagrams and they are as follows:

- **CARD DIAGRAMS** are known as the **FULL DEAL** when all four hands are displayed with 13 cards dealt to each of the four players. Card diagrams can be 4-hand, 3-hand, 2-hand and a single-hand card diagrams.

- **BIDDING DIAGRAMS** illustrate the complete bidding sequence from the opening call in the first round to the last bid, which is always followed by three consecutive passes. In *Enjoy Beginning Bridge*, the learning process is facilitated by starting the Bidding Diagram with West continuing clockwise in compass-point order: North, East and South.

- **PLAY DIAGRAMS** display each of the 13 tricks in the exact order in which they are played; also, they show the number of the trick played (1-13); the side that won each trick; and, a running tally of the tricks won by each side

CHAPTER 3

POINT-COUNT SYSTEMS: HAND VALUATIONS AND COUNTING SURE WINNERS

"HOW HIGH AND WHERE" SHOULD THE BIDDING GO

We now address the two basic questions involved in making any bid: "how high" and "where" should the bidding go? The first question refers to the levels of the bids which promise to make from 7 tricks to 13 tricks; and, which one of the 5 strains will be selected as the trump suit or Notrump. The bridge skill needed to determine how high the bidding can go is based on the ability to value a hand's trick-taking strength. Since this chapter is dedicated to **POINT-COUNT SYSTEMS,** the counting of points in a hand, its primary focus is the "how high" part of a bid; with the "where" part deferred until Chapter 4.

DETERMINING THE TRICK-TAKING POTENTIAL OF A COMBINED HAND

HAND VALUATION estimates a single hand's trick-taking potential and is usually performed twice in a deal before the dummy becomes visible; the first is immediately after player receives his 13 cards; and, from the Bidding Conversation when he gains information regarding the other side's Holdings. When the bidding is over and the dummy is visible, it is the first time the **DECLARER,** the first player to mention the strain in which the contract is played, has visibility of his side's **COMBINED HAND**. This is declarer's "moment of truth" because it is now possible to count the **SURE WINNERS,** cards that will surely win tricks, when led without losing a lead and compare that **TALLY** to the number of tricks promised in the auction. While the Tally is made after the bidding has ended, it remains important because it determines, with some certainty, the number of extra tricks, if any, needed to fulfill a contract.

DECLARER VALUES HIS HAND

For now, the focus is on the declarer's valuation of his own hand. Since tricks are most frequently won by High Cards, a point-count system is used assigning 4,3,2,1 **HIGH CARD POINTS (HCPS)** respectively to the Ace, King, Queen and Jack for a total of 10 HCPs. However, trick-taking potential does not come solely from HCPs; 5-card or longer suits are also a source for making tricks. Recognizing that fact, the point-count system adds one **LENGTH POINT (LP)** for a 5-card suit; a 6-card suit can add 2LPs and so on. When length points are added to High Card points that *blend of points* are described as **VALUATION POINTS (VPs).**

RESPONDER, AS LIKELY DUMMY, REVALUES HAND WHEN 8-CARD MAJOR FIT IDENTIFIED

The first time **RESPONDER** values his hand for trick-taking purposes he uses HCPS and LPs in a valuation known as the **INITIAL POINT-COUNT**. When responder, raises the opening bid to at least the 2-level he usually identifies at least an 8-card fit in the combined hand. At that point, the Responder becomes the likely dummy and revalues his hand for Shortness, a 2-card suit or less. This revaluation involves adding 5, 3, or 1 point when holding a void, singleton or a doubleton, respectively. These points are known as **DUMMY POINTS (DPs),** points in lieu of LPs. Once the likely dummy's hand has been revalued with DPs, the FINAL **POINT-COUNT** has been established for the Responder, the likely dummy.

THE PERFECT BRIDGE HAND

The "Bridge-Logic" for assigning a point value to shortness reflects the fact that the fewer non-trump cards held in a hand the more the number of trump cards are likely to be held in that hand. That is why A **PERFECT BRIDGE HAND** is defined as one that will produce 13 tricks if played in Notrump irrespective of the opening lead or the composition of the other three hands. This is one example of such a hand

$$A\ K\ Q\ J\ x\ x\ x\ x\ x$$
$$A\ K$$
$$A$$
$$A$$

As you will see, the reason why Shortness is good when game is in a trump suit is the same reason why it is a liability in Notrump, which depends on Length to make tricks when there is no risk of being trumped.

THE BEGINNER'S BIDDING LADDER

A problem facing bridge pioneers was the need to graphically provide Guidelines, in the form of required point-count ranges for making specific levels of bids. For example, it is a Law of Contract Bridge that the lowest bid on the bidding ladder that can be made is at the 1-level, promising to make at least 7 tricks, the first 6 tricks of which are known as **BOOK** and do not count towards game. For example, if you bid 1-notrump and make 7 tricks you only earn points towards game for 1 trick. So, while the first 6 tricks do not count, they need to be made. It's the Law!

The highest bid on the Bidding Ladder is the 7-level, promising 13 tricks and known as a **GRAND SLAM**. The range of points needed between levels 1 and 7 is displayed in a graphic known as the **BIDDING LADDER**, aptly termed since each higher level bid requires an increasing number of tricks and an increasingly higher range of points.

At the end of this Chapter, we introduce as Figure # 1, the Beginners' Bidding Ladder which is calibrated to show the number of tricks and point-count ranges a beginning bidder should hold in order to successfully bid at each of the 7 levels. The Beginners' Bidding Ladder also shows that different **GAME CONTRACTS** require different point-counts: Notrump requires 25 VPs; a major requires 25-26 VPs; and, a minor requires 29 VPs. Further, for each of the 7 levels, the 5 strains are arrayed in ascending order, starting with Clubs and ending in Notrump. As a result there are 35 calibrations in the bidding ladder.

COUNTING SURE WINNERS IN A COMBINED DUMMY-DECLARER HAND

Once the Declarer has visibility of the dummy, a much more precise method becomes available to the declarer for evaluating the trick-taking potential of the combined hand. That process involves counting Sure Winners, tricks that will be surely made without losing the lead. The Matrix at the end of this Chapter provides the guidance needed to acquire that skill; one that is indispensable in **DECLARER PLAY,** in which the Declarer controls the play of both the dummy and his own hand. The **OPENING LEAD,** the first card played by defense is the cue for the dummy hand to be made visible.

In addition to Sure Winners, there are also **DELAYED WINNERS,** those cards that will surely win tricks, usually starting with the second time the suit is led. For example, if your combined hand holds the KQ of a suit, but not the Ace, the King becomes a winner once you make a **SACRIFICE PLAY,** in which you lead your Queen to the Ace. In *Enjoy Beginning Bridge*, we value the KQ sequence in a combined hand as ZERO sure tricks, only because the trick-taking ability of the KQ sequence is delayed until the Sacrifice Play draws out the Ace, at which time the KQ become 2 winners.

EXPERIENCING HAND VALUATIONS

In Quiz # 1, following this chapter, we provide a number of hands dealt to the opening bidder. Your assignment is to determine if you can make an opening bid using initial point-count guidance. The goal of this drill is to enable you to make valuations in a fairly rapid manner. What's the rush? Remember, you have three other players waiting for you to make the opening bid so that they can get on with their assigned roles in the auction. There is a tempo in bridge and it is a dedicated beginner who recognizes that fact of bridge play.

CHAPTER 3
MATRIX

COUNTING SURE WINNERS

FROM HONOR CARDS IN A COMBINED HAND	SURE WINNERS (a)
AKQJ10 Sequence, same suit	5
AKQJ Sequence, same suit	4
AKQ Sequence, same suit	3
AK Sequence, same suit	2
AQ, same suit	1
A, singleton	1
KQ sequence, same suit	0
KJ, same suit	0
QJ, same suit	0
J10, same suit	0

FROM GOOD 6+-CARD SUITS IN A SINGLE HAND	PLAYING-TRICKS (b)
Good 8-card suit	7
Good 7-card suit	6
Good 6-card suit	5

FOOTNOTES

(a). SURE WINNERS, IN A COMBINED HAND: All the single suit, combined Dummy-Declarer hands shown below hold 5 Honor Cards, the AKQJ10 except for Hand # 5 which holds 4 Honor Cards. The maximum number of sure winners a combined hand can produce is usually determined by the length of the cards in the declarer. Since the cards are distributed randomly to both the Dummy and the Declarer, the 4 combined hands can appear in a number of different shapes and produce a number of different winners.

#1	#2	#3	#4	#5
Dummy	Dummy	Dummy	Dummy	Dummy
J10	AJ10	Q	Void	J10
Declarer	Declarer	Declarer	Declarer	Declarer
AKQ	KQ	AKJ10	AKQJ10	KQ

The maximum number of sure winners within a suit in a combined Dummy-Declarer hand is usually but not always limited to the length of the cards in the hand of the Declarer. In Combined Hand #1 above there are three sure winners (AKQ); in Combined Hand #2, note there are 3 sure winners (the AKQ) with only delayed winners in the Declarer; in Combined Hand #3 there are four sure winners(AKQJ); in Combined Hand #4, there are five sure winners (AKQJ10); and in Hand #5 there are Zero winners.. In *Enjoy Beginning Bridge,* we do not count half-tricks such as 1.5 sure winners for the AQ or 0.5 winners for a singleton King as some guidance suggests. While half-winners are authorized, it is believed that the added complexity of half-points distracts the beginner more from the learning process than it adds to it. Obviously, *this count of sure winners is only available after the dummy becomes visible.*

(b). PLAYING TRICKS are expected winners in a single hand holding a good 6+card suit. For example, KQJ10987 is a good 7-card suit that will yield 6 tricks once a **SACRIFICE** is made so that the remaining 6 cards become sure tricks. Not all hands need to make a sacrifice; for example, the A K Q J 10 9 8, when held by the opening leader with play in Notrump suit, will surely make 7 tricks.

CHAPTER 3
FIGURE # 1

THE BEGINNERS' BIDDING LADDER

"How High & Where" Bid Levels	Trick- Strains	Score	Contracts	Valuation Point Guidance
7-Level (13 tricks)	7-Notrump	220		
	7-Spades	210		
	7-Hearts	210		
	7-Diamonds	140		
	7-Clubs	140	**Grand Slam, very rare**	**37+VPs and 13 tricks**
6-Level	6-Notrump	190		
	6 Spades	180		
	6 Hearts	180		
	6-Diamonds	120		
	6-clubs	120	**Small Slam, rare**	**33+VPs and 12 tricks**
5-Level (11 tricks)	5-Notrump	160	Rare, Natural	29+VPs and Game bonus
	5-Spades	150	Rare, Natural	29+VPs and Game bonus
	5-Hearts	150	Rare, Natural	29+VPs and Game bonus
	5-Diamonds	100	Game in minor	29+VPs
	5-Clubs	100	Game in minor	29+VPs
4-Level (10 tricks)	4-Notrump	130	Rare, Natural	26-28VPs, and Game bonus
	4Spades	120	Preempt opening	0-12VPs Good 8+Spades
	4 Hearts	120	Preempt opening	0-12VPs Good 8+Hearts
	4-Diamonds	80	Preempt opening	0-12VPs Good 8+Diamonds
	4-Clubs	80	Preempt opening	0-12VPs Good 8+Clubs
3-Level (9 tricks)	-Notrump	100	**Game, Natural**	25+VPs Balanced
		90	Preempt opening	0-12VPs Good 7+Spade
		90	Preempt opening	0-12VPs Good 7+Heart
		60	Preempt opening	0-12VPs Good 7+Diamonds
	3-Clubs	60	Preempt opening	0-12VPs Good 7+Club
2-Level (8 tricks)	2-Notrump	70	Game Invitational	20-21HCPs & Balanced Shape
	2-Hearts	60	Weak-2 Preempt opening	5-10VPs Good 6-card spade suit
	2-Spades	60	Weak-2 Preempt opening	5-10VPs Good 6-card heart suit
	2-Diamonds	40	Weak-2 Preempt opening	5-10VPs Good 6-card diamonds
	2-Clubs	40	**Strong Artificia**	**22+VPs, No shape requirement**
1-Level (7-tricks)	1-Notrump	40	Natural, partscore	15-17HCPs, Balanced Shape, Stoppers
	1-Spade	30	Natural, partscore	13-21VPs &any 5+card spade suit
	1-Heart	30	Natural, partscore	13-21VPs & any 5+card heart suit
	1-Diamond	20	Natural, partscore	13-21VPs & any 3+card diamond suit
	1-Club	20	Natural, partscore	13-21VPs & any 3+card club suit

Notes: Since *Beginning Bridge* includes weak and preemptive suit openings at Levels 2-4; the only exception is the 2-club opening bid, a conventional bid signaling a powerful 22+VP hand. All other suit bids in Levels 2-4, signal weak hands and **GOOD 6-8-CARD SUITS**, with two of the top three or three of the top five honors. Notrump openings at Levels 1-5 are always natural openings but at levels 4-5 opening bids in Notrump are very rare. Levels 2-4 are reserved for weak, preemptive suit openings and the 2-club artificial strong opening. All 1-level openings are natural and very common. Preemptive openings are always made one or more levels higher than necessary. The 5-level suit opening bid, in a minor is natural, signals 29+VPs promising 11 tricks. A 4 level major suit opening would be natural but very rare. *Enjoy Beginning Bridge* caps the bidding at the 3-level in Notrump; 4-level in a major; and 5-level in a minor because it does not include Slam Bidding. This ladder shows bids at Levels 6 and 7 because, with a Perfect Bridge Hand, Slam Bidding skills are not required.

CHAPTER 3
QUIZ # 1
HAND VALUATIONS

SCENARIO: Make an opening bid if the guidance permits; or, pass if you cannot. Minimum opening strength for a 1-level suit bid is a point-count range of 13-21 VPs; and 15-17 HCPs for a 1-notrump opening. In this quiz, your opening bid is limited to the "How High" part of the bid. The guidance required for choosing the "Where" part of the bid will be introduced in the next chapter. ***Note that spot cards are designated with an "x" since the ranks of spot cards are not needed for hand valuations.*** Since the 10 is also an Honor Card, it will be shown as "10" rather than "x" when it is important to identify a good 5-card or longer suit. For example a "good 5-card suit requires two of the top three or three of the top five Honor cards, which includes the 10 card. **Finally, in *Enjoy Beginning Bridge*, the suits are always arrayed in descending rank order: Spades, Hearts, Diamonds and Clubs.**

```
                K Q x x
                K J x x x
                J x x
                A
```

Analysis # 1: You will open at the 1-level. This unbalanced 5-4-3-1 shape holds a 15 VP initial point-count derived from 14HCPs+1LP for the 5-card suit. This is within the bidding ladder's point-count range of 13-21 VPs which permits a 1-level suit opening. If this bid becomes the final bid, it will require 7 tricks.

```
                x x x
                x x x
                x x x
                x x x x
```

Analysis # 2: You will pass. Probably, the ugliest, perfectly balanced 4-3-3-3 shape you will ever see; Zero HCPs, Zero LPs and only one long suit, the 4-card Clubs. Be mindful of your proprieties and do not grimace as you make your call. Since all the cards are 9-card spots or below, you have just been dealt a Yarborough. The odds of such a miserable hand being dealt are 1,827 to one.

```
                A K x x
                A Q x x
                A 10 x x
                A x
```

Analysis # 3: It's so sad! You have four Aces in a hand with a total of 21 HCPs, but will not be able to play it because you have 14 cards in your hand, a misdeal. Because you failed to count your cards immediately after they were dealt to you face-down, the hands must be thrown in, reshuffled and re-dealt by the same dealer. This time Lady Luck may not treat you so kindly

CHAPTER 3
QUIZ # 1, CONTINUED
HAND VALUATIONS

Q J 10 9
Q J 10 9 x
Q J
Q J

Analysis # 4: You will open at the 1-level. This unbalanced 5-4-2-2 shape has 13 VPs, derived from 12 HCPs+1LP for the 5-card Hearts, enough to make an opening bid since it is within the 13-21 VP range. The problem is that all the high cards are Queens and Jacks, known as "Quacks" with no trick-taking ability of their own, if led. While the temptation may be to pass, do not forget that bridge is a partnership game and your partner may find this hand supportive for what he holds. For example, the fact that both your major suits are long suits (4-cards or more) is an important quality. *Also, it is a maxim of bridge that nothing happens until someone makes a bid.* The guidance says you need 13 VPs to open and that is what you have. Obviously, you will need to be cautious and keep the bidding low, especially since a point-count of Sure Winners gives this hand a Zero! *Lessons Learned: While this hand has 13 VPs, more experienced players would open at the 1-level only if it has the 10 and 9 in the major suits, even though these two cards do not contribute to the point-count.*

A K Q x x
x
J x x x x
Q x

Analysis #5: You will open at the 1-level. This unbalanced 5-5-2-1 shape has 14 VPs, derived from 12 HCPs+2LPs from the two 5-card suits. With 14 VPs you are within the 13-21 VP guidance for an opening at the 1-level. In the next chapter we discuss the guidance for choosing between the two 5-card suits.

K Q J x x x
x x x x
x
x

Analysis #6: You will open preemptively at the 3-level in a suit: This very unbalanced 7-4-1-1 shape has a good 7-card Spade suit and 9 VPs derived from 6 HCPs+3LPs in the 7-card suit. Usually, the only point-count required to open preemptively at level-3 and level-4 is "less than opening strength," Based on that guidance, this hand is preemptive since its strength is weak and primarily derived from its "good" 7-card suit. The main value of this bid is that it is high enough to interfere with the other side's bidding since a suit overcall will need to be made at the 4-level. Two important features of this particular shape are the singletons which are valuable because, when they become void, the holder of this hand can take a trick with a trump card when the other side leads a Diamond or a Club.

CHAPTER 4

FIRST SEAT DETERMINES THE "WHERE" PART OF THE OPENING BID

In the previous chapter, we restricted an opening bid's description to the "How High" part of the bid. While that facilitated the teaching of the point-count system, it was not realistic since a legal bid must always include a strain as well as a bidding level. For example, an opening bid of 1-heart indicates both the level of the bid as well as the suit proposed as trump, Hearts. While the "How High" part of a bid is important since it governs the number of tricks the contract promises, *it is the right to select the strain that is the real prize since whatever strain the Auction's winners choose, you can be sure that it is usually bad news for the defense.*

WHERE YOU SIT IS WHAT YOU ARE CALLED

Bridge players assume four different identities, depending on the roles assigned to their seats: The First Seat opens the bidding; the Second Seat challenges the opening bid by overcalling or doubling; the Third Seat, with support, responds to the first seat's opening bid or without Support introduces **NEW SUIT,** one that is unbid; and, the Fourth Seat **ADVANCES** the second seat's overcall or takeout double. While the dealer always assumes the role of the First Seat, his **CALL,** any Bid, Double or Pass, may be a Pass. When a Pass occurs, the opportunity to open the bidding goes to the dealer's Left Hand Opponent (LHO). If the LHO opens the bidding, he becomes the First Seat and the bidding continues in compass-point direction.

THE PRIORITIES WHEN CHOOSING THE "WHERE" PART OF THE OPENING BID

A Notrump opening bid is always preferred over any other opening bid because it more precisely describes the opener's shape and strength than an opening bid in a suit. However, Notrump is not the Responder's first priority for the Play of the Tricks. The "Bridge-Logic" for that anomaly is derived from observations showing that ***play in a major suit with an 8-card or longer fit will usually yield one or more tricks than play in Notrump, whether it's played in part -score or game***. This guidance is an important part of beginner's ongoing bridge strategy and priorities for selecting major suits as trump suits. Beginners, mark this page for reference purpose, you will need to refer to this guidance many times during your play as a beginner.

When a hand is not suitable for an opening in Notrump, the second priority is to open in a major; and, the last priority is an opening bid in a minor suit. Minors are ranked last because their game contract requires 11 tricks, one trick less than a Small Slam. Because of the higher number of tricks required, relative to major suit and Notrump openings, minor suit contracts carry the highest risk not being fulfilled.

OPENING BIDS AT THE ONE-LEVEL

While opening bids can be made at any of the 7 levels on the bidding ladder, the most common opening bid level is at the 1-level because it gives the Responder, maximum **BIDDING SPACE,** in which to respond.

OPENING BIDS IN NOTRUMP

A hand **SUITABLE FOR NOTRUMP** is balanced; has a narrow range of 15-17HCPs; and, at least three of its suits are **GUARDED,** suits headed by any High Card, known as a **STOPPER** and followed by a specified number of spot cards, known as **GUARDS**. The mission of a Guarded Suit is to prevent the Opening Leader from making a run of tricks in a suit.

While the guidance prefers 3 guarded suits, it may sometimes be acceptable to open in Notrump with only 2 guarded suits. Specifically, it is acceptable when the 2 guarded suits are major suits. Once the opening in Notrump is made, *opener's partner knows more about the combined hand than the opener and is in the best position to determine how "High and Where" their bidding should go.*

A Notrump opening bid is a **LIMIT BID** because it places a limit on the hand's strength. For example, when the bidding agreement requires 15-17HCPs for a 1-Notrump opening bid that bid limits to 17 HCPs the maximum number of points that hand will show. Another example would be the 2-spade response in the 1-spade---pass---2-spade bidding sequence. The 2-spade response is a limit bid which signals 3-card support and a limited hand of 6-10 VPs. When an opening bid is limited, the responder will know more about the combined hand than the opener. As a result there is little need to bid further in order to describe the strength and distribution of a combined hand.

The guidance for opening in 1-Notrump is as follows:

- Any one of the three defined balanced shapes: 5-3-3-2, 4-4-3-2 or 4-3-3-3
- An opening point-count range of 15-17HCPs
- Preferably, at least three of the four suits headed with Stoppers backed up by Guards

A guarded suit is headed by a High Card Stopper, followed by a specified number of spot cards (Guards). The number of Guards required to back up a Stopper is determined by the rank of the High Card Stopper: for example, an Ace needs none; a King needs one; a Queen, two; and, a Jack, three.

Here are some examples of hands that are preferred for an opening in notrump and one that may be acceptable:

(A)	(B)	(C)	(D)	(E)	(F)
4-4-3-2	4-4-3-2	5-3-3-2	4-3-3-3	4-3-3-3	5-3-3-2
AQ52	96	AJ1074	AKQ	AKQ	KQ
AQ8	AK5	K43	J5432	AKJ10	KQJ
K4	KQ106	K106	Q108	432	432
Q843	KQ53	KQ	A42	842	AJ1074

Hand (E), while not preferred because there are only 2 guarded suits, is acceptable since the 2 guarded suits are major suits. All the other hands (A, B, C, D and F) have at least three guarded suits.

WHEN A BALANCED HAND CAN BE OPENED IN NOTRUMP OR IN A MAJOR

With the 5-3-3-2 shape in Hand (C) above, holding 5-card and 3-card major suits, the guidance is to open the bidding in Notrump. With the same 5-3-3-2 shape and 5-card and 2-card major suits, the guidance is to open the bidding in the 5-card major suit. When a 5-3-3-2 shape does not have a 5-card major, such as in (F) above the alternative is always to open in Notrump.

WHEN A HAND IS TOO STRONG FOR A 1-NOTRUMP OPENING

When holding a balanced hand with more than 17HCPs, a hand too strong for opening in 1-notrump, you may open in a suit since the upper range of that guidance is 21VPs. However, with 20-21HCPs, a balanced hand and preferably 4 guarded suits, you can open naturally in 2-notrump, a non-forcing, strong opening. The term "preferably 4 guarded suits" indicates that, with a 20-21HCP range, it is worth the risk of playing with only three guarded suits.

THE HAZARDS OF PLAYING IN NOTRUMP

When play in a major is not available, responder to a Notrump opening will usually prefer to play in Notrump over play in a minor suit. In Notrump, "happiness" is leading a Long Suit where a run of tricks are more likely to be made since there is no risk of being trumped. For that reason, the declarer's "nightmare," when playing in Notrump, is the opening leader who parleys a run long enough to accumulate enough tricks to defeat the contract *before the declarer has a chance to gain the lead.* In the end, while Notrump is a great opening bid, the priority is for responder to get the side to play in a major suit.

OPENING THE BIDDING IN A MAJOR SUIT

When an opening in Notrump is not available, the second choice, opening in a major requires the following: an initial point-count in a range of 13-21VPs and any 5-card or longer major suit. This Guideline identifies the **BIDDING SYSTEM** as **5-CARD MAJORS, BEST MINOR,** primarily used in the U.S. Let's look at a hand, albeit an extreme example, with the shape and strength that qualifies for an opening in a major suit:

```
x x x x x
K Q J x
A Q x
A
```

This unbalanced 5-4-3-1 shape has 17 VPs, derived from 16 HCPs+1LP from the 5-card Spades. Since the guidance for an opening in a major suit is "any" 5-card or longer suit, the all spot, 5-card spade suit is within the Guideline and the opening bid may be in 1-spade. While the all-spot Spades may look like a liability, your Opening Bid in 1-spade conforms to your Bidding Agreement Discussion and that is the essence of good bidding. Obviously, if your partner has Support for your Spades, he will be disappointed with your Spades. However, if your partner does not like Spades and suggests Hearts as a New Suit, you will still have a shot at an 8-card fit in a major suit.

CHOOSING THE "BEST MINOR" WHEN OPENING IN A MINOR

Since you and your partner have agreed to play "5-Card Majors, Best Minor," there comes a time when you simply cannot open the bidding either in Notrump or in a major; and, your only option is to open in your "Best Minor." The guidance for selecting the right minor suit is as follows:

- With two 5-card minors, always open the higher ranking one
- With two 4-card minors, always open the higher ranking one
- With a choice of two 3-card minors always open the lower ranking one, Clubs (1)
- Never open in a minor with a 2-card suit
- With two minor suits of different lengths, always open the longer minor suit---"length before strength".

(1) There is an exception to that rule: with 3 spots in Clubs and the AKQ in Diamonds, the choice is Diamonds.

Note that the minor suit selection is usually based on the rank of the suit relative to the other minor; the point-count of the suit does not apply. The only exception, when holding two 3-card minor suits, is to open in Clubs. Let's look at a hand in which it makes good sense to open in a minor at the 1-level:

```
x x
x x x
A K Q J x x
A K
```

This very unbalanced 6-3-2-2 shape has an initial-point-count of 19VPs derived from 17 HCPs+2LPs from the 6-card Diamonds. With this hand, since neither an opening bid in Notrump nor in major meets guidance, you will bid 1-diamond because Diamonds are your ranking 3-card or longer minor. With the opening in 1-diamond, there is much Bidding Conversation required before the side can determine their best and final bid. In fact, Responder's priority is to find a major suit fit in the combined hand. If that is not possible, then the default priority is to play in Notrump. Lastly, if you have no choice but to play in a minor, it is likely that the final contract will be in a **PART-SCORE** rather than in game, requiring 11 tricks.

STRATEGY AND TACTICS FOR OPENING BIDS

Since nothing happens in bridge until someone makes an opening bid, the guidance to the First Seat is to make every attempt to open the bidding within the parameters of his bidding agreement. To that end, the following applies:

- With 15-17 HCPS and a balanced hand, the first priority for opening the bidding is in Notrump. Since the Notrump opening is a Limit Bid, signaling a strength level of limited range, it makes it easer for the side to find the best contract. A game bid in Notrump requires at least 25 VPs and promises 9 tricks.

- With 13-21VPs, a balanced hand, a 5-card or longer major, and unable to open in Notrump, you should open in a major suit at the 1-level. A game bid in a major requires at least 25-26 VPs and promises at least 10 tricks.

- With 13-21 VPs, but unable to open in Notrump or in a major suit, the only option left is an Opening Bid in a minor suit. The minor suit requirement is a 3-card or longer minor suit. With a choice between the two minor suits, the longer minor suit is opened; open 1-club with two 3-card minor suits. The Guideline for a game bid in a minor is at least 29 VPs and promises 11 tricks.

- With a **STRONG HAND,** over 20 VPs, there are two **STRONG OPENING BIDS** that can be made at Level-2, without being recognized as Weak Two openings:

    Open in 2-notrump with 20-21HCPs and 3-guarded suits, preferably 4 guarded suits; a non-forcing invitational bid. With 25 VPs, and a balanced hand an opening in 3-notrump is very rare and may be confused with a Conventional bid. Note there are no Preemptive Openings in Notrump since all Notrump bids are **NATURAL,** reflecting the character of the Hand.

    Open in the Artificial Strong 2-club opening with 22+Vps This conventional bid is **FORCING.**

- With **SUB-MINIMAL STRENGTH,** in the 10-11 HCP range, there is guidance that permits 1-level Natural openings of suit bids using the "Rule of Twenty" discussed below. Natural opening suit bids made at Level 2 are restricted to the **WEAK-TWO** openings with good 6-card suits and 5-10 VPs. Those made at Levels 3-4 with good 7-card or 8-card suits respectively and less than opening strength are descriptive and considered **PREEMPTIVE.**

- **SLAM BIDS,** made at Levels 6-7, promise 12-13 tricks and require at least 33 VPs or 37 VPs for a Small Slam or a Grand Slam, respectively. When a combined hand holds 33+VPs, beginner may be tempted to *consider* bidding a Small Slam. For example, if the opening bid is 2-notrump, signaling 20-21 HCPs and Responder holds more than 13VPs, the combined hand has at least 33 VPs, the strength required by the bidding ladder to make a Small Slam bid. However, simply holding 33 VPs is not, by itself, sufficient justification for committing to a Small Slam contract that permits the defense to defeat the contract with only 2 tricks.

- With 33 VPs, if the defense holds two of the four Aces and play is in Notrump, defense, which always has the Opening Lead could get **FIRST ROUND CONTROL** of those two suits and make 2 tricks before the Small Slam bidder gets to make his first lead! (Note, when a side has 33 HCPs, the other side cannot have 2 Aces since the total HCPs in the 2 sides would be 41 HCPs; an impossible total since the maximum number of HCPs in a deal cannot exceed 40 HCPs).

  With 33HCPs, however, if the other side has the AK of the suit, then, while the 40 HCP maximum is not exceeded the other side could take 2 tricks and defeat the slam bid. The skill required to identify the location of Aces, is an advanced bidding skill, considered beyond beginning bridge. As a result, final bidding by beginners is capped: at the 3-level when bidding game in Notrump; 4-level when bidding game in a major; and, the 5-level when bidding game in a minor.

  Also, there is no scoring advantage in a Rubber format to bid beyond these three capped levels since the **TOTAL POINT-SCORE** is based on tricks made, not on tricks bid and made. Further, tricks bid but not made can be costly, resulting in ZERO points scored and penalty points awarded to the defense.

When none of the opening bid options are available; there is always the dreaded "Pass," the most difficult word in bridge.

THE CONTROVERSIAL RULE OF TWENTY FOR OPENING SUIT BIDS

With 10-11 HCPs, beginner may consider the controversial **RULE OF TWENTY,** which permits a hand with slightly less than opening strength to make an opening suit bid. To use the Rule of Twenty, the total *number* of cards in the two *longest suits* when added to the number of HCPs in the hand, must add up to at least 20. For example, if you have 11 HCPs and your two longest suits have at least nine cards, your total is 20; alternatively, with only 10HCPs, your two longest suits must have at least 10 cards so that your total is also 20. The Rule of Twenty should be used with caution since it is made with a point-count that is less than Opening Strength and may fail in the play.

The following are two examples of hands that may be opened using the Rule of 20 and one hand with which you should pass:

OPEN (1)	PASS	OPEN (2)
A J 10 x x	K Q x x x	x
A J 10 x x	K Q x x x	A Q J x x x
x x	x x	K x x x
x	x	x x

With the hand under the "OPEN (1)" column there are two good 5-card major suits and 10 HCPs. This is an excellent hand to open using the Rule of 20 because of the potential for identifying at least an 8-card major suit fit; and, activating delayed winners in the 2 major suits. With the hand under the "PASS" column, you also have 10HCPs and two 5-card major suits, neither of which are "good;" and, in which, neither suit has a sure winner. Even if partner was able to identify an 8-card fit, without an Ace in the combined hand you will have difficulty making a low level contract.

A second relatively safe hand to open with the Rule of 20 is the hand under the "OPEN (2)" column. While it only has 1 good major suit, the suit is a 6-card suit headed by an Ace with the potential for making more than one trick. The hand's two longest suits total 10 cards and the hand's point count includes 10HCPs. In the end, even with strong support from a responder, bidding should be kept at a low level. As with all Guidelines, following the Rule of 20 blindly can get you in trouble. For that reason the Rule of 20 has few supporters in bridge literature and should be used with caution.

WHEN A HAND'S SHAPE, NOT POINT-COUNTS, DETERMINES AN OPENING BID

Sometimes, relying only on point-counts to open the bidding may get the beginner in trouble. Frequently, the shape of a hand may be more important than the hand's point-count.

POINT COUNT	SHAPE
K Q	A J 10 x x
K Q x	A 10 x x x
Q J x x	x x
x x x x	x

With the hand under "POINT COUNT," relying only on point-count guidance, you will usually open in your "best minor,"1-diamond. If you are forced to play this hand in a 1-diamond contract, you will have a challenge because this hand has Zero sure winners; and most of the High Cards are Queens and Jacks, known as "Quacks" Similarly, relying on point-count guidance only, you might pass the 5-5-2-1 "SHAPE" hand with 11VPs derived from 9HCPs+2LPs. However, if you count Sure Winners this hand has at least 5-6 sure tricks once you activate your Delayed Winners. Also, since the hand has a singleton and a doubleton, suits which can be quickly rendered void, permitting additional trump tricks. So, what's a beginner to do? To open the "POINT -COUNT" hand with zero sure tricks while disregarding the "SHAPE" hand that single-handedly promises more tricks makes no sense. Brent Manley, in *The Tao of Bridge* answers this beginners' dilemma as follows: "**…many of the "rules" you encounter are more Guidelines than unbreakable standards. Learn to tell the difference."**

THE STRATEGY OF PREEMPTIVE OPENING SUIT BIDS AT LEVELS 2-4

With less than Opening Strength, guidelines permit an opening suit bid to be made at levels 2 to 4 when holding a good 6-card to 8-card suit, respectively. These opening bids are considered as both Interfering and Preemptive. Further, these bids are also considered Natural because their bid guarantees some holding in the suit bid. At the two-level, Weak-Twos, in any suit except Clubs, only need 5-10VPs; and, any good 6-card suit. (The 2-club opening is reserved for the conventional strong opening). At the 3 and 4-levels Preemptive Openings can be made in any suit, require less than opening strength (0-12 VPs) and, good long suits: a 7-card suit at the 3-level or, at least a good 8-card suit at the 4-level.

There are three basic reasons for making obstructive and preemptive opening suit bids:

- Permits an opening suit bid at the 2-level or higher with less than Opening Strength;
- May be obstructive enough to discourage bidding that is makeable or encourage bids that are not makeable;
- Very descriptive and precise bids permitting responder with strength to raise the opening bid

PLAYING THE PREEMPTIVE OPENING SUIT BID---TAKING THE OFFENSIVE

When the Preemptive bidder is forced to play in his weak hand, the prevailing wisdom is that he will lose because the other side likely holds the majority of the High Card Points. So, why would you make a preemptive opening bid when the expectation is that you may lose in the play? Briefly, the Preemptive Opening presents a dilemma of choices: you can make a **SACRIFICE BID** in which you will lose; or, you can pass and let the opponents score points by playing in a contract acquired cheaply in a non-competitive auction. The solution to this dilemma requires a brief tutorial on **SCORING** and the **TRADE-OFF ANALYSIS** that considers the costs of both choices and permits you to resolve this dilemma by choosing the least expensive alternative for your side.

A BRIEF TUTORIAL ON THE SCORING PROCESS AND TRADE OFF-ANALYSES

The skill needed to resolve the Preemptive bidding dilemma requires the ability to make a **TRADE-OFF,** place a cost on the two outcomes so that the least expensive one can be identified. To do that, the **TRICK-SCORE POINTS (TSPs)** awarded to the defense, if the Preemptive contract is defeated, must be compared to the TSPs awarded to the Declarer if the Preemptive contract is fulfilled. If defeat will result in a loss of fewer points than letting the other side take the contract, then there is logic in making Sacrifice or Preemptive Bids and losing in the Play.

The next step is to determine the TSP value of a successful game bid: estimated to usually be about 500 points. *Therefore, if your goal is to interfere in the other side's attempt to successfully make a game contract, you would not want to lose more than 500 points, the number of points they would usually earn if they make game.*

The final step is to calculate the number of tricks you can afford to lose. These tricks, known as **UNDERTRICKS,** are the deficit between the tricks required by your Preemptive bid and the tricks actually made. For example, if your opening bid is at the 4-level, requiring 10 tricks and you only make 7 tricks, you will have gone down 3 Undertricks which result in **PENALTY POINTS** awarded to the defense.

The Penalty scored for three Undertricks, in a worse case scenario, is between 500TSPs and 800TSPs awarded to the opposition. The worse case depends on whether your side is **VULNERABLE,** has already won a game and your side holds a **CONTRACT DOUBLED FOR PENALTY,** a bid which doubles the penalty TSPs awarded to the other side if you fail to make your contract. So, if the other side would only make 500TSPs in a successful contract, you would not want to "pay" more than 500 TSPs to prevent that outcome.

There is a "rule" to handle this Tradeoff, known as the **RULE OF TWO AND THREE:** it suggests you not go down more than two tricks if you are Vulnerable when you have won a game and not go down more than three tricks if you are Non-Vulnerable, when you have not yet won a game.

In summary, Preemption is a double-edged sword: it can be a powerful tool for cheaply Interfering with the other side's ability to bid successfully; and, it can also be an expensive tool if you do not keep your bidding in check. Preemptive Opening bids, while rare, are presented for your consideration because they provide an excellent training opportunity to challenge your skills in the game's three major transactions: the Bidding, the Play and the Scoring.

STRONG OPENING BIDS

ARTIFICIAL, STRONG 2-CLUB OPENING SUIT

When holding 22+VPs, you are too strong for an opening suit bid at the 1-level. The guidance is to open in 2-clubs, a Conventional Bid, with a defined meaning understood by the partnership. Of course, once you and your partner agree to use the 2-club bid, you have precluded your side from making "weak-two" bids in Clubs. Finally, the 2-club Conventional bid is **FORCING,** requiring partner to respond.

THE 2-NOTRUMP OPENING BID

The 2-level Notrump opening bid has all the features of the 1-level notrump opening bid, while requiring 20-21HCPs, a balanced hand and preferably stoppers in all 4 suits. The 2-notrump opening does not preclude partner from identifying a major suit fit in the combined hand using the Stayman or a Transfer. Because of its high point-count requirements, beginner will find the 2-notrump opening a rare event. Finally, Notrump openings at any level are never preemptive because they always require strength.

TRANSLATING HAND VALUATIONS AND SHAPES INTO OPENING SUIT BIDS

In Quiz # 2, at the end of this chapter, we provide sample hands and a "commentary" that provides more than just "correct" answers. If these quizzes are realistic they will provide you with the experiences necessary to develop the skills and instincts needed to make the best possible opening bids. Following each commentary there is a "Lessons Learned" section that provides observations that go beyond the specific quiz problems. The Beginners' Bidding Ladder in Chapter 3, as Figure #1, is an important resource for the beginner to develop his bidding skills.

CHAPTER 4
MATRIX

CHOOSING BETWEEN OPENING BIDS IN NOTRUMP AND OPENING SUIT BIDS

The First Priority: Opening bid in Notrump

    With a defined Balanced Hand and

- 15-17HCPs and stoppers and guards in 3 suits, open 1-notrump
- 20-21HCPs and stoppers and guards preferably in all 4 suits, open in 2-notrump

The Second Priority: When Notrump opening is not available open in a Major

    With 13-21VPs and any 5-card or longer Major

- Open in the Major at the 1-Level

The Third Priority: When Notrump or a Major Suit opening bid is not available open in a Minor:

    With 13-21VPs

- Open in the best Minor 3-card or longer suit, never open in a doubleton

Notes:

The above priorities are a constant throughout Enjoy Beginning Bridge. With these priorities in mind: an opening in a minor is better than a pass since it gives the opener another shot at arriving at a major contract after partner responds. Responder only needs a 4-card major suit and 6+VPs to introduce a major as a "new suit" alternative to the minor suit opening..

Opening strength is defined as the point-count range of 13-21VPs. The range is further defined as follows:

- **Minimum opening strength**: with 13-16VPs
- **Medium opening strength**: with 17-18VPS
- **Maximum opening strength**: with 19-21VPS

The "Best Minor" is the longest minor of the two available suits. With two 4-card minor suits, open in Diamonds; and, with two 3-card suits open in Clubs. Make sure this guidance is in your bidding agreement.

CHAPTER FOUR
QUIZ # 2
VARIETIES OF OPENING BIDS

SCENARIO: You are the dealer, the first to open the bidding. You and your partner have agreed to play 5-Card Majors, Best Minor. Your bidding agreement includes all the opening bids discussed in this Chapter. In this scenario, you will be dealing with the selection of both bidding levels and strains. Also, you will be dealing only with initial point-counts since the bidding conversation has not yet progressed beyond the opening bid. Since a fit has not yet been identified, Dummy Points are not involved in these hand valuations. What is your call with the following hands?

A x x x x
K Q 10 x x
x x
A

Commentary # 1: You will open at the 1-level in Spades: This unbalanced 5-5-2-1 shape has an initial point-count of 15VPs (**Minimum Opening Strength**) derived from 13HCPs+ 2LPs for the two 5-card major suits. While the opener's first priority is to open the bidding in 1-notrump that option is not available since the hand is not suitable for Notrump. Opener's second priority is to open with at least a 5-card major and 13-21VPs. *Lessons Learned: With opening strength and two 5-card major suits, select the higher ranking major regardless of the strength in the lower ranking major.*

A K Q J
K J 10 x x x
Q x
x

Commentary # 2: You will open at the 1-level in Hearts: This unbalanced 6-4-2-1 shape has a strong initial point-count of 18VPs placing it in the Medium Opening Strength category. The strength is derived from 16HCPs+2LPs for the good 6-card Heart suit. The 1-heart opening signals 13-21VPs and at least a 5-card suit. The opening convention provides no way of signaling to your partner that you hold more than a 5-card major; and, more than Minimum Opening Strength. If you open in 2-hearts, you will mislead your partner because you have agreed that a 2-heart opening bid signals a hand weak in strength with 5-10VPs and a good 6-card suit. While you have the good 6-card suit, you are certainly not weak. *Lesson Learned: With 2 major suits of different lengths, the guidance is to open in the longest suit since that should result in the longest suit in the combined hand. At this point, you have done all you can to describe your hand to your partner. Clearly, there is more bidding conversation to be held before a final bid is made. With 18VPs and some support from partner, your side could be close to a game bid.*

Q x x
A K x
K x x x
A Q J

Commentary # 3: You will open in 1-Diamond: This very balanced 4-3-3-3 shape, with 19HCPs is in the Maximum Opening Strength range (19-21VPs). You are too strong for an opening in 1-notrump; too weak for an opening in 2-notrump; and, you have no 5-card major. Your only option is to bid your longest and senior ranking minor suit, diamonds. *Lesson Learned: while an opening in a minor suit is your last priority, you have no choice but to do so since any other bid would violate your bidding agreement. You have done all you can by correctly bidding your best minor. Partner's priority, even with support for the minor suit bid is to identify an 8-card or more fit in a major.*

CHAPTER 4
QUIZ # 2 CONTINUED
VARIETIES OF OPENING BIDS

```
A K J x x
x x
Q x x
K Q x
```

Commentary # 4: You will open in 1-Spade. This 5-3-3-2 balanced shape has an initial point-count of 16VPs derived from 15HCPs+1LP for the 5-card Spades. You have two choices with this hand: you can open the bidding in 1-spade; or, you can open in 1-notrump since the point-count and balanced shape requirements are met. *Lesson Learned: The guidance is to open the bidding in 1-notrump when the second major is a 3-card suit and in the 5-card major when the other major* **is in a 2-card suit.**

```
x x x x
A Q x x
K Q x
x x
```

Commentary #5: You will pass: While this balanced 4-4-3-2 shapes has an initial point-count of 11 HCPs, it is too weak for an opening bid at the 1-level in a suit or in Notrump. The Rule of Twenty is not available since the two longest suits do not add to nine cards. *Lesson Learned: the only alternative to making a pass is to make a bid that would mislead your partner and seriously erode his confidence in your ability to deliver what you bid. A pass does not always mean that your hand is worthless. It only means that it does not fit any bid included in your bidding agreement. This is one of the most important lessons in bridge; so, keep it in mind! If you were in the Pass-Out seat, this is a hand that you might consider bidding, especially with two 4-card majors.*

```
K x x
A x x x
K Q x
A x x
```

Commentary # 6: You will bid 1-notrump: This perfectly balanced 4-3-3-3 shape has 16HCPs with stoppers and guards in all four suits. This hand could also be opened in a minor suit, Clubs, the "best minor suit." *Lesson Learned: Your first priority is always to open in Notrump ahead of a minor since game in Notrump requires only 9 tricks and yields the same trick-score points as game in a minor, requiring 11 tricks. It also provides a more precise description of your hand in terms of strength and shape.*

```
A K x
A K x x x
K Q x
A x
```

Commentary # 7: You will bid 2-Clubs, the artificial 2-club strong opening bid: This balanced 5-3-3-2 shape with 24VPs derived from 23HCPS+1LP for the 5-card Heart suit is too strong for a 1-level opening in a suit; and, too strong for a 2-notrump opening. This hand is very close to game. *Lesson Learned: the artificial 2-club strong opening suit bid requires 22+VPs and is the only option available to show your powerful hand. Your partner is forced to respond.*

CHAPTER 4
QUIZ # 2 CONTINUED
VARIETIES OF OPENING BIDS

```
x x x
x x
x x
K Q J x x x
```

Commentary # 8: You will pass: This 6-3-2-2 unbalanced shape has only 8VPs derived from 6HCPs+2LP for the good 6-card Club suit. You are too unbalanced and too weak for a Notrump opening or any opening suit bid at the 1-level. You would like to open with a Weak-Two bid in clubs but that is not possible since the 2-club opening is reserved for the strong artificial opening bid. ***Lesson Learned: this is a good example of the need to follow the bidding agreement. Once again, it is better to pass than to mislead your partner by bidding what is not in your hand.***

```
A K x x x
x
x
A K Q J x x
```

Commentary # 9: You will open in 1-Club: This interestingly unbalanced 6-5-1-1 shape has 20VPs derived from 17HCPs+3LPs for the 5-card spade suit and the good 6-card club suit. You are too unbalanced for a 2-notrump opening bid. Since you are at the Maximum Opening Strength range for a 1-level suit opening, the only question remaining is the suit choice. ***Lesson Learned: While you always want to play in a major, select the longest suit since that should result in the longest suit in the combined hand and more tricks. Selecting a minor suit for an opening does not preempt your partner's priority to identify an 8-card or more major fit. The two singletons are very valuable when playing this hand in a trump suit since they can be quickly voided.***

```
A K x
A K Q
K x x
Q x x x
```

Commentary # 10: You will open the bidding in 2-Notrump: This 4-3-3-3 balanced shape has 21HCPs and stoppers in all four suits. While you could also open in a minor at the 1-level, the 2-notrump opening is a better bid since it signals a strong hand and balanced shape. ***Lesson Learned: with a 2-notrump bid, the responder is provided with the clearest indication possible regarding the opener's strength and shape. However, play in Notrump is not the side's first priority. With a 5-card suit available in a major and no point-count requirement, the Responder can use the Transfer bid to identify an 8-card major suit fit. That would be the most desirable outcome since play in a major with an 8-card fit will usually yield more tricks than play in Notrump, whether it is played in part-score or in game. If the Transfer bid is not available, a Stayman could be used with a 4-card major and 8 or more HCPs.***

CHAPTER 5

THE MECHANICS OF THE BIDDING PROCESS

There are three major acts in the play of bridge: the Auction's bidding process, the Play of the Tricks, and the Scoring of the points earned in the Play of the Tricks. While each act is an indispensable part of the overcall game, it has been estimated that bidding impacts 90% of the game's outcome. Good bidding makes for winning bridge since it selects the strain that is right for your side and only promises a number of tricks that can reasonably be made. Bad bidding, picking the wrong strain or bidding at a level that is too high, can be fatal.

THE KEY TO THE BEGINNING BRIDGE BIDDING CONVERSATION'

For beginners, the most unique feature of the Bidding Process is the protocol that allows the opening bidder to fairly accurately describe to his partner (and the other side) the Shape that he holds and its trick-taking potential. The only problem is the limitation on the words that can be used during the Bidding Conversation: restricted to 14 words: the 7 numbers (Levels 1 through 7); the 5 strains (Spades, Hearts, Diamonds, Clubs and Notrump); and, "Pass" and "Double." That's it; a 14 word menu and not one word more!!

Another challenge of the Bidding Conversation is that the word "Double" can mean "for Takeout" or "for Penalty." The bidders must determine which type of Double is intended by its location in a Bidding Round. Except for the Opening Bid, any bid other than the Double must be of a level legally higher than the preceding bid. For example, an opening in 1-spade can be overcalled at the 1-level by no less than a bid of 1-notrump.

COMPETITIVE VERSUS NON-COMPETITIVE AUCTIONS

The Auction involves four players bidding for the right to define the **CONTRACT,** to specify the number of tricks required and the strain in which the game is played. **COMPETITIVE AUCTIONS,** when both sides enter the Bidding Process usually involves, for beginners, only one or two rounds of bidding. When one side does not bid, rendering an Auction non-competitive, the other side's goal is to simply determine, their "best contract" by having a Bidding Conversation between themselves. Of course, even in a non-competitive Auction, the other side is privy to the Bidding Conversation and obtains important information about the bidding side's Hand Shape and trick-taking potential.

With 4 consecutive passes in the first Round, the bidding is ended; and, in all other rounds 3 consecutive passes are required to end the bidding and define the final contract.

HOW THE AUCTION STARTS AND HOW IT ENDS

The **BIDDING PROCESS,** also called the Auction, starts when the First Seat completes valuing his hand's strength and makes an Opening Bid. However, even with that bid, the Auction is not yet competitive until the Second Seat Overcalls or Doubles for Takeout. Now, the Third and Fourth Seats have their own bidding assignments: the Third Seat's job is to Support the opening bid and the Fourth Seat's job is to Support the overcall or Takeout Double.

When all four seats make a call, a **BIDDING ROUND** is completed, but the bidding continues; and, in as many Rounds as is necessary until one side determines it has made its best and final bid. After 3 consecutive passes, the **BIDDING SEQUENCE** is over and the contract is Defined..

THE "BILL OF RIGHTS" OF THE BIDDING PROCESS

LAW # 41 of Contract Social Bridge, of special interest to the beginner, states "….Declarer, before he plays from the dummy, or either defender, at his first turn to play, may require restatement of the Auction in its entirety." This right is important, because suits mentioned by the opponents represent valuable intelligence and the beginner should not consider it an inconvenience to make this request. Further, even after it is too late to have the Auction completely restated, Declarer or either defender is entitled to be informed what the contract is and whether, but not by whom, it was Doubled for Penalty.

The other item of interest to the beginner is the **ALERT.** This is a single word, not a Call, when one player announces to his RHO that his partner's bid is a Convention, one with a defined meaning understood by the partnership. The only exception to this propriety is when the Conventional bid is so well known, such as the Stayman response to a Notrump opening, that it is unnecessary to announce an Alert..

While Conventions are a code between partners, they cannot be a secret; and, must be disclosed to the opponents. To avoid that appearance, the "Alert" is used to ensure the opponents are aware that a Conventional Bid was made so that they can determine if they need an explanation of the meaning of the bid.

THE BEGINNERS' BIDDING AGREEMENT

The "glue" that keeps both the Bidding Process and a partnership together is the **BIDDING AGREEMENT**, an understanding between the partners as to what Conventions and Signals will be used and what they mean.

The foundation of a bidding agreement is that a bid must reflect what the bidder holds. An embarrassing moment in bridge is when the dummy is laid out and the declarer asks his partner, "Where is the hand that you bid?" When partners develop trust, they become a formidable team. One way of strengthening a partnership, especially a new one, is to spend some time, rehearsing each other's understanding of various bids, Signals and Conventions. Only when the partnership has had significant experience playing together, is it considered **ESTABLISHED,** with little need for such discussions; except, of course, when introducing new Conventions.

When partners play for the first time, a **BIDDING AGREEMENT DISCUSSION** is essential to successful play. To that end, a scripted conversation between two first-time partners is presented below. While you may not be familiar with some of the terms used, since they may not yet have been introduced, the important point is to get the feel for how you would hold such a discussion with a new partner and how you would describe what you know and, also, what you do not know.

Finally, the bidding agreement is not a legal written document signed by the two partners and witnessed by a notary. Rather, *it is a conversation between two beginners who are playing as partners for the first time. This agreement is not static and should be reopened whenever guidance changes. The discussion includes the Bidding System they use (5-card Majors, best Minor, for example), the Conventions they use and the bridge skills they have acquired (the Jacoby Transfer, for example) as well as those bridge skills they have not yet mastered, Slam Bidding for example.*

TWO NEW PARNERS: THEIR BIDDING AGREEMENT DISUCSSION

New Partner # 1: "Hi, I'm Andy My first priority, when I am the opening bidder, will be to open the bidding in Notrump because it's the best way to describe a hand's shape and strength. If that's not possible, my second choice is to open the bidding in a 5-card major suit with 13-21VPs because we make more points if we have an 8-card fit; and lastly, I'll open in my best minor. Very rarely, I may open light in a major with only 12 points but only if I have a 5-card suit. My thinking is that it is better to open the bidding than to pass and leave you guessing as to what, if anything, I have in my hand. By the way, a Notrump opening doesn't just mean a balanced hand and 15-17 High Card Points; if we intend to play in Notrump, we need stoppers and guards in at least three of the suits.

Just because I open the bidding in Notrump doesn't mean that I expect to play in it. As I said, playing in a major suit with an 8-card or longer fit usually yields more tricks than playing in Notrump, whether it's played in part-score or game. Hopefully, you will be able to suggest a major suit that will fit with what I am holding. If we can't play in a major, we should play in Notrump with a suitable hand rather than a minor suit because less risk is involved.

If you open in 1-notrump and I have a 5-card major, I will make a Jacoby Transfer in diamonds or hearts depending on what my major suit is. Remember, I will make a Transfer even if I have zero points. If I can't make a Transfer and have one or two 4-card majors and eight or more High Card Points, I will bid a Stayman, looking for a 4--4 match in a major. We should rehearse the Bidding Conversation that's used when the Stayman is bid.

If I can't open in Notrump or in a major at the 1-level, our 5-card American Majors bidding system allows us to open in our "best minor" with 13-21VPs. If I open in a minor at the 1-level, I am showing opening strength and most likely a 4-card suit; but, if that's not available, the least I will open with is a 3-card minor suit because that's better than passing while holding opening strength. I expect that we will usually stop the bidding of the minor at the 4-level because a part-score in a minor is still better than bidding Game in a minor and going down one.

My bidding style reflects my belief that nothing happens unless one of us opens the bidding. So, I will open most any way I can. Don't get the wrong idea, my bids will reflect my hand's strength. All I'm saying is that while I will try to open, you can be sure it always will be in a responsible manner. That includes using the Rule of Twenty, which some people think is not responsible bidding because it has less than opening strength. With less than opening strength, I may use any of the three preemptive opening suit bids at the 2-4 levels requiring a good 6-8 card or more suits, respectively. By the way, I define a "good" suit as one that has two of the top three or three of the top five honors.

So, if I open at the 2-level in any suit except Clubs, that is a Weak Two and it means I hold less than opening strength and most of my strength is in one good 6-card suit. If I open at the 3-level, it means I hold less than opening strength and a good 7-card suit. Oh, I almost forgot to ask if you understand the Law of Total Tricks. It's an especially good bidding guide for determining "how high" a side should bid in a competitive auction. While there's more to it; simply stated, you usually bid to the level of your side's number of trumps. We will need to spend some time rehearsing the Law.

Opening with a weak-two means you and I can never open in 2-Clubs unless we mean it to be the Convention for a strong hand signaling 22 or more points. Even though that kind of a hand is rare, we should probably rehearse the strategy for responding to a 2-club opening in case we get lucky. My understanding of the guidance for responding to a 2-club opening, when holding 8+VPs, is to show a good 5-card suit in a major at the 2-level or at 3-level with a good 5-card minor; or, with a balanced hand suitable for Notrump bid 2-notrump. When none of those options are available, we should use the 2-diamond Artificial Waiting Bid which does not deny 8+VPs. This provides opener with maximum bidding space to describe his hand.

Since I'm just a beginner, my Conventions are not all that fancy. As I have said, I can do a Stayman and a Jacoby Transfer to find a major suit fit. I love the double for takeout because it does not mention a suit or a bidding level but signals opening strength and promises at least 3-card support for whatever unbid suit you select as the trump suit.

My 1-level suit overcalls of 1-level suit openings will signal a good 5-card suit or more; at least 7 to 17 HCPs; and, will always be made at the 1-level even if I have enough points for a 2-level suit overcall. That way, you should have enough bidding space to make your rebid.

Like most beginners, I have not yet mastered Slam Bidding because it requires advanced Conventions such as the Blackwood and Gerber. Also, I suggest we do not bid higher than game level, whether it's a game contract in a major, in Notrump or in a minor. That's because in Rubber Bridge our Total Point-Score is based on tricks made even if they are more than what was bid.

When I'm in the Fourth Seat and advance in a cuebid to your suit overcall, I am simply telling you that I have 10 or more points and 3-card or more support. You will need to let me know whether your overcall is a maximum level or minimum level overcall.

All my opening leads will come from the Leads section in the Convention Card which I received from the ACBL. I use it often and it's fairly easy to identify the opening lead card the Convention Card recommends because it's the one in bold. You can have this one since I have a number of them. If you are the opening leader I will use the "Attitude Signal:" if I like your suit I will play a High Card and if I don't, I'll play the low card. By the way, the Rule of Eleven is a great tool if we are playing defense and you are the declarer's RHO.

Oh, and this is important: if I pass, it doesn't always mean that I have a weak hand. I could have opening strength without a bid that describes my hand. So, if you are in the fourth seat with two passes to you, I'll understand if you balance with a bid that has fewer points than what the guidance calls for.

I almost forgot: Since I'm a beginner I avoid the double for penalty, unless it is blatantly obvious that the other side cannot make their contract. Also, I'm not all that clear on what kind of a hand I am supposed to have in order to make a double for penalty. I have finally learned how to score in a Rubber format, so I'll take care of that for us.

I'm sure I've forgotten something but that's all I can think of right now. Is there anything you want to add?"

New Partner #2: "Thanks, Andy, it sounds like we are about on the same skill level. I appreciate that you have kept the number of conventions to a reasonable level for beginners. I don't think I'll have any problem following your bidding system. If you use the Stayman and I don't have a 4-card major, I'll rebid in 2-diamonds indicating that a fit is not possible. When I'm the opening leader, I'll open in a suit you have bid, unless, of course, I have a more powerful one. If I'm the Declarer, I will need a minute or two to analyze the dummy, count sure tricks and determine how many extra tricks if any we will need to make our contract. Also, if I don't understand a bid the other side makes, I will ask them to explain it when it is my turn to bid. Some players don't like it when beginners do that, but it's important to know what's happening, especially when we are playing with more experienced players.

As you, I have yet to master Slam Bidding; you know, where they ask each other for Aces and Kings. I agree that we should keep our final bids at whatever game contract we are bidding. Your strategy about making an opening bid whenever possible is the way to go. I noticed that you did not mention the **RULE OF 15,** that's when the first three players pass; and, the fourth player with slightly less than opening strength determines if his HCPs plus the number of Spades held add to 15 or even 16; if they do, an opening bid should be made naturally.

I assume you don't mind playing "penny a point." Let's have some fun and see if two beginners can give these two Intermediate players a run for their money. By the way, my name is Felice.

CHAPTER 6

THE SECOND SEAT REACTS TO THE ENEMY'S OPENING BID

Some of you may object to my use of the term "Enemy" to describe those nice people on the other side of the bridge table. While "nice people" they may be, once the bidding becomes competitive, it is war between the two sides. Winning the Auction war means one side gets to select their best suit as the trump suit and the losers simply dance to the winners' tune. Winning is fun; losing is not!

The opening bid made by the First Seat was introduced in Chapter 4 as a bid of many different varieties. We now introduce the challenges the other side may make to the opening bids, usually by the Second Seat. Actually, there are only two varieties of challenges: the **OVERCALL,** a call made immediately after an opening bid; and, the **TAKEOUT DOUBLE** a bid with opening strength asking partner select one unbid suit as trump..

THE SUIT OVERCALL DANCES TO THE OPENING SUIT'S TUNE

Let's start with the most common overcall, the suit overcall, made immediately following an opening bid. If the Opening Bid is in a suit at the 1-level, the suit overcall can also be at the 1-level, but only if the overcall's strain outranks the opening suit bid; and, if it is a good 5-card or any 6-card or longer suit. For example, if the opening bid is 1-club, a 1-level suit overcall can be made in any one of the three other suits: Spades, Hearts or Diamonds, all suits that outrank Clubs. Obviously, when the opening bid is 1-diamond, a 1-level suit overcall can only be made in a good 5-card or any 6-card or longer Spade or Heart suits, the only two that outrank Diamonds.

When the opening bid is 1-spade, the only overcall that can be made at the 1-level is 1-notrump; and, all suit overcalls must be made at the 2-level with 13-17VPs. Because a 2-level suit overcall is challenging a 1-level suit opening bid, it requires the strength equivalent for opening the bidding.

Suit overcalls are always referred to as **SIMPLE SUIT OVERCALLS** when they are made at the **CHEAPEST LEVEL AVAILABLE,** the lowest bid that is both legal and not higher than necessary. Stated another way, a Simple Suit Overcall can be at the 1-level or the 2-level. In the end, the rank and level of the suit overcall is highly dependent on the rank and level of the opening suit bid.

SIMPLE SUIT OVERCALLS AT THE ONE AND TWO LEVELS

An important bidding feature is the concept of Overcalling at the cheapest level. For example, if an opening bid is in 1-diamond and the overcaller has 7-17VPs with a good 5-card Heart suit or any 6-card or longer Heart suit, the guidance permits an Overcall in 1-heart, a simple suit overcall, even if the Overcaller has 17VPs, the top of the point-count range. If the Opening was in 1-spade a 2-level suit Overcall in Diamonds, Clubs or Hearts would require Opening Strength, 13-17VPs and a good 5-card or any 6-card or longer suit. This 2-level suit overcall is also a simple suit overcall since it is made at the cheapest legal level.

WHY OVERCALL AN OPENING BID?

Usually, you will Overcall to create **INTERFERENCE** within the bidding and possibly encourage the other side to bid higher than they should; or, more happily, you have a good opening hand that you would have opened if you were the First Seat. At the very least, the Overcall is an opportunity to show partner your best suit, one he can use as an Opening lead suit.

WHEN AN OPENING BID IS BEST LEFT UNCHALLENGED

While this may sound counter-intuitive, there are times when the opening suit bid is not only liked by the Second Seat, but best left unchallenged. Usually, a suit that is good for the Opener is not good for the other side. This dilemma occurs because the 5-card Majors bidding system permits opening in a major in *any* 5-card major suit. When that guidance is taken literally, an Opening Bid can be made with a 5-card suit made up, for example, of all Heart spot cards. So, if you as the Second Seat hold the AKQJ Heart sequence, and the opening bid was 1-heart with a 5-card all spot suit, you hold four sure winners in a trump suit proposed by the other side. With that strength, you should be able to set a contract that requires 10 tricks. Don't expect to see this happen very often. This strategy is called a **TRAP PASS**.

PREEMPTIVE OVERCALLS

There are no Preemptive Overcalls in Notrump because Notrump bids, whether they are opening bids or overcalls, always have strength. For that reason preemptive suit overcalls are simply referred to as Preemptive Overcalls; bids which always have a good long suit and a weak hand. The OEB defines a Preemptive Overcall as defensive, usually made with a double or triple **JUMP**, a bid made one or two levels higher than needed, aimed at obstructing the bidding. Consider the following hand in the Second Seat *when the First Seat opens in 1-heart, signaling 13-21VPs and at least a 5-card suit:*

```
A J 10 x x x x x
x
x x
x x
```

This hand, with only 5HCPs does not meet the guidance for a Simple Suit Overcall in 1-spade because it does not hold the required 7-12HCPs. However, it does hold a good 8-card Spade suit, has "fewer than 10" and meets the guidance for a Preemptive Overcall at the 4-spade level, a Triple Jump of a 1-level opening. If the intent is to obstruct the other side's bidding, the 4-level Spade overcall is clearly more effective than the 1-spade overcall. At the same time, this 4-level Overcall leaves little Bidding Space for partner in the Fourth Seat to advance in Spades, hardly likely, since it would require a 5-level bid. The only question remaining is whether the opening side will Double for Penalty the 4-spade contract.

The effectiveness of Preemptive Suit Overcalls is that they can be made with weak hands; obstructing the other side's bidding by taking up bidding space. However, its use also comes with the same risk as that of a Preemptive Opening: the possibility that the other side may pass and the overcaller plays the weak hand, likely doubled for penalty.

2-NOTRUMP OVERCALLS, NO! TAKEOUT DOUBLES YES!

The 1-notrump Overcall, like the 1-notrump opening Bid, provides a relatively precise description of a hand's strength and shape. Guidance for the 1-level Notrump overcall is more stringent, requiring 15-18HCPs, balanced hand, *length and strength in the opening suit bid* and stoppers in 2 of the other suits. This added stringency is needed to protect against a run likely started with the Opening Lead card in the Opening suit bid. If that suit was unguarded, with no stoppers, it would be difficult to get the lead back to the Notrump overcaller. *There is no guidance provided for a 2-Notrump overcall* because a better bid is the more flexible Double for Takeout, discussed below.

THE DOUBLE FOR TAKEOUT

The Double for Takeout, made with Opening Strength, usually by the Second Seat, immediately following an opening suit bid is a Convention asking partner to select the trump suit while promising him at least 3-card support and preferably 4-card support for any *unbid* suit partner selects. Since the double has no upper limit, it is an excellent alternative to the suit overcall which is capped at 17VPs. So, when the Second Seat is too strong for a suit Overcall, the Double permits a challenge to the opening suit bid without mentioning a suit or taking up bidding space. Since the Doubler is the likely dummy, he can revalue his hand for shortness using Dummy Points (void-5; singleton-3; and, doubleton-1) in lieu of length points. The possibility of a Double immediately following an Opening Suit bid being mistaken for a Penalty Double is remote.

ACCEPTABLE SHAPES FOR THE DOUBLE FOR TAKEOUT

The following four shapes may be used when bidding a Double for Takeout: with the first two shapes preferred; the third shape is acceptable but not preferred because it offers fewer opportunities for providing 4-card support than the first two shapes which are preferred; and, the last shape, while the least preferred is still acceptable, for reasons explained below:

- 5-4-4-0
- 4-4-4-1
- 4-3-3-3
- 4-4-3-2

The ability of the doubler to provide partner with at least 3-card support for any unbid suit depends on the opening suit bid. For example, after *an opening bid of 1-diamond,* consider this hand's suitability for a Double:

- Q x
- K Q x x
- K J x x
- Q x x

This hand is not suitable as a Takeout Double because Spades, one the 3 unbid suits, will only provide 2-card Support if selected by the Doubler's partner. Since this hand does not meet the Guideline's requirement that any unbid suit selected will provide at least 3-card support, it is not acceptable.

Here is the 4-3-3-3 shape to consider for a Double when opening, in 1-diamond:

- K Q x x
- Q x x
- K x x
- A K Q

This is a perfectly balanced 4-3-3-3 shape with no Shortness (Void, Singleton or Doubleton) and 19HCPs. Since Diamonds have been bid, partner's selection is restricted to the best unbid suit among Spades, Hearts and Clubs. In this case, any unbid suit selected will result in at least 3-card support and possibly 4-card support. As a result, while suitable, this hand is not preferred because it only has one unbid suit that can provide 4-card support.

BIDDING A DOUBLE FOR TAKEOUT WHEN IN THE FOURTH SEAT

While the above examples of doubles for takeout were all made by the Second Seat, there is nothing in the guidance to preclude the double being made by the Fourth Seat after both opponents have bid and partner has passed. The only difference is that when the Fourth Seat makes the double, there may now be only two unbid suits from which the Second Seat can select as a trump suit.

CHALLENGING NOTRUMP OPENING BIDS WITH SUIT OVERCALLS

When the Opening Bid is in 1-Notrump, the Second Seat can challenge the opening with a 2-level suit Overcall, holding at least a good 5-card suit within a range of 13-17 VPs. However, when the opening bid is in 2-notrump, a rare event, requiring 20-21HCPs, the cheapest legal bid for a suit overcall will be at the 3-level, requiring 9 tricks. Beginner should be wary of getting too high in the bidding. Since there are 3 players who have not bid and only 19HCPs remaining, it will be difficult for the overcaller's side to prevail in terms of point-count.

MATRICES AND QUIZZES

We complete this chapter on the role of the second seat with matrices that provide guidance for suit and notrump overcalls. We also offer quiz problems which include commentaries and lessons learned sections. The quiz scenario places beginner in the Second Seat, playing defense, responding to an opening bid with simple suit overcalls, preemptive suit overcalls, notrump overcalls as well as the double for takeout.

CHAPTER 6
MATRIX

SUIT AND NOTRUMP OVERCALLS

OPENING BID	SECOND SEAT CHALLENGES WITH AN OVERCALL OR A DOUBLE
1-club	Simple suit overcall: overcall at cheapest level with 7-12HCPs or 13-17VPS and 5+ good diamond, heart or spade suit.
	Notrump overcall at level 1: balanced hand, 15-18HCPs, Length and Strength in opponent's suit, Stoppers and Guards in at least two other but preferably in the other 3 Suits
	Double for Takeout: 13VPs, no upper limit and a shape promising at least 3-card support in any one of the three unbid suits (Diamonds, Hearts or Spades)
	Preemptive jump suit overcall at 2-level, 5-11VPs and a good 6-card Diamond suit or any good 6-card major
	Preemptive jump suit overcall at 3-4 level with any good 7-8 card suit respectively and 0-9Vps
1-diamond	Simple suit overcall: at cheapest level with 7-12HCPs or 13-17VPs and any good 5+ major suit. All other options basically the same as shown in 1-club opening bid
1-heart	Simple suit overcall: at cheapest level with 7-12HCPs or 13-17VPs and good 5+ spade suit
	Simple suit overcall at 2-level, 13-17HCPs, any good 5+minor suit
	All other options same as shown 1-club and 1-diamond openings
1-spade	Simple suit overcall at 2-level, 13-17VPs, any good 5+minor or 5+hearts
	All other options same as in all opening bids shown above
1-notrump	Simple suit overcall at 2-level, 13-17HCPs, any good 5+card suit
	Preemptive overcalls at the 3-level or higher after a Notrump opening are not recommended. Since a Notrump opening promises limited strength, they may double, leaving you with a contract requiring 9 tricks which you likely will not make.

Footnote: The above strategy for challenging opening bids is basically the same, regardless of the opening bid, with the exception that the legal rankings of the strains must be observed. For example, the guidance for challenging a 1-diamond opening is different from challenging a 1-club opening bid.

CHAPTER 6
QUIZ # 3
SECOND SEAT REACTS TO OPENING BIDS

SCENARIO: AFTER THE FIRST SEAT OPENS WHAT IS REACTION FROM SECOND SEAT?

SCENARIO # 1: FIRST SEAT OPENS IN 1-CLUB

> A K J x x
> A x
> K x x
> K J x

Commentary # 1: You will double. This balanced 5-3-3-2 shape with 20VPs is too strong for a 1-level suit overcall or a 1-Notrump overcall; further, the shape is not one of the four acceptable shapes for a double since selecting Hearts as the unbid suit does not provide at least 3-card support. Nevertheless, bidding a double with this shape is better than passing with a hand this strong. With this strength, the Second Seat is more interested in making game than in simply obstructing the bidding. The double asks partner to select a trump suit from one of the three unbid suits. *Lessons Learned: When holding strength, the Second Seat's overriding priority is to keep the bidding alive. The use of the forcing double, even when it is made with a shape that does not promise at least 3-card support for any of the three unbid suits, signals opening strength and gives partner an opportunity to select a trump suit. While it is possible that the partner may select the 2-card Heart suit as trump, subsequent rebids can show the good 5-card Spades or a hand suitable for Notrump.*

SCENARIO # 2: FIRST SEAT OPENS IN 1-HEART

> x x
> K x
> A Q 10 x x x
> A x x

Commentary # 2: You will overcall in 2-diamonds: This unbalanced 6-3-2-2 shape has 15VPs derived from 13 HCPs+2 LPs for the good 6-card Diamonds. Your only available legal option is a simple suit overcall of 2-diamonds which requires 13-17VPs and a good 5-card or longer Diamond suit: *Lessons Learned: Your minor suit overcall has accurately described your opening strength as well as your best suit for opening lead purposes. While play in a minor suit is not your first priority, the overriding priority is to accurately describe your hand to your partner as well as challenge the opening bid.*

> A K J x x
> x x
> x x x
> x x x

Commentary # 3: You will overcall the 1-heart opening with a simple suit overcall in 1-spade: This 5-3-3-2 balanced shape has 9VPs. You are within the minimum overcall point-count range of 7-12HCPs for a 1-level simple suit overcall. With a good 5-card suit in Spades, your overcall meets the guidance for an overcall at the cheapest level available. *Lessons learned: You can do no more. You have interfered in the bidding, accurately described your hand within the confines of your bidding agreement and provided maximum bidding space for your partner. At some point in the auction your partner may need further bidding conversation to determine if your overcall was made with Maximum or Minimum strength.*

CHAPTER 6
QUIZ # 3 CONTNUED
SECOND SEAT REACTS TO OPENING BIDS

SCENARIO # 2: CONTINUED

x x
A K Q J 10
x x x
A K x

Commentary # 4: You will pass the opening bid in 1-heart. This 5-3-3-2 balanced shape holds 18VPs. The opening bid in 1-heart signals a 5-card Heart suit and 13-21 VPs. You love Hearts as the other side's trump suit since you have length and strength in the opponent's suit. *Lessons Learned: If the final contract is in 1-Heart, the declarers must make 7 tricks. A count of sure winners in only your hand tallies to 7 sure winners (5 winners in Hearts and 2 in Clubs). Of course, the final determinant will be your skill in the play of the tricks. This pass is known as a "Trap Pass."*

SCENARIO # 3: FIRST SEAT OPENS 1-DIAMOND

K Q x x
K x x x
x
K Q 10 x

Commentary # 5: You will double the opening bid of 1-diamond. This 4-4-4-1 unbalanced shape has an initial point-count of 13HCPs and is one of the two preferred shapes for a double since it has 3 unbid suits that can promise at least 4-card support. Since the opening bid is an accommodating 1-diamond bid, this hand can promise 4-card support for any of the three unbid suits (Spades, Hearts and Clubs). *Lesson Learned: Within the confines of your bidding agreement, the takeout double is your best challenge to the opening bid.*

A J x
K Q x
K Q x x
K J x

Commentary # 6: You will double the opening bid of 1-diamond: This 4-3-3-3 perfectly balanced shaped has an initial point-count of 19HCPs. Without a good 5-card suit, a suit overcall at any level is not available; and, the hand is too strong for an overcall in 1-notrump. This double's shape promises at least 3-card support for the three unbid suits (Spade, Hearts and Clubs). *Lessons Learned: This hand is close to game and the double keeps the auction alive.*

CHAPTER 6
QUIZ # 3 CONTINUED
SECOND SEAT REACTS TO OPENING BIDS

SCENARIO # 4: FIRST SEAT OPENS IN 2-HEARTS

```
x x x
A x x
A K J 10 x
J x
```

Commentary # 7: You will pass the opening bid in 2-hearts: This balanced 5-3-3-2 shape has an initial point-count of 14VPs. The 2-heart opening bid is a Weak-Two, signaling 5-10VPs and a good 6-card Heart suit. While you barely have enough strength to double, your hand's shape is not one of the four acceptable shapes. You do have the 13-17VPs and the good 5-card suit for a 3-diamond overcall, requiring 9 tricks. *Lessons Learned: While a 3-level overcall is the cheapest overcall available, it may be too high a price to interfere, especially if you think the opening bid is not makeable. What you can deduce about Hearts is that the first two seats hold 9 Hearts (6 in the opener and 3 in the second seat) and the third and fourth seats have 4 Hearts between them. If these two hands split evenly, the opener will barely make his 8 tricks. Since there is bidding conversation to come, the safest course at this point may be to pass.*

SCENARIO # 5: FIRST SEAT OPENS IN 1-NOTRUMP

```
x
K Q x x
K 10 x x
K Q x x
```

Commentary # 8: You will pass the opening in 1-notrump: This 4-4-4-1 unbalanced shape, with 13HCPs, is one of the 2 preferred shapes for a double. However, since the only logical double, following a notrump opening bid is a penalty double, this is not a bid you would choose at this point since it is too early to determine with confidence that a 1-notrump bid cannot be made. A simple suit overcall at the 2-level is not available since that requires opening strength and a good 5-card suit. *Lessons Learned: While it is difficult to pass with an above average 13HCP hand, it is better to disappoint your partner with a pass than to mislead him with a bid that is not in your bidding agreement. Especially when it is one that could result in a double for penalty, a bid not in the beginners' skill set.*

```
x x
K Q x
K 10 x
A K 10 x x
```

Commentary #9: You will overcall the 1-notrump opening with a 2-club bid: This balanced 5-3-3-2 shapes holds 16VPs derived from 15HCPs+1LP for the good 5-card Clubs. Since the opening is 1-notrump, the cheapest legal overcall is at the 2-level in a good 5-card or longer minor suit with 13-17VPs. The Club suit meets this requirement. *Lessons Learned: If this was an opening hand, you would have opened in 1-club. There is much bidding conversation remaining. This is the best you can do with what you now know.*

CHAPTER 6
QUIZ # 3 CONTINUED
SECOND SEAT REACTS TO THE OPENING BIDS

SCENARIO # 5 CONTINUED

```
x x
A Q 10 x x x x
x x x
x
```

Commentary # 10: Your bid, following the 1-notrump opening depends on where your side is in the Rubber Scoring format. With 9VPs, less than opening strength, you are too weak to open in a double; and, your 7-card long suit is too long for a 2-heart overcall. With "fewer than 10" and the good 7-card Hearts, the guidance permits preemptive double jump overcall in 3-hearts. Your guidance also permits you to pass. *Lessons Learned: Just because guidance permits obstruction does not mean that you must obstruct. Actually, the guidance is to obstruct only if the price you pay for that obstruction is not more than what the other side would have earned if you did not obstruct the bidding. The best guidance for that dilemma is the Rule of Two and Three: do not go down more than 2 tricks if vulnerable and 3 tricks if non-vulnerable. So, the first question is how much does the other side need to make game? If they already have some TSPs below the line, they may not need to bid and make game in Notrump. You should also consider that it is highly likely they will double your contract. If you are still motivated to interfere with the bidding, you should make the 3-heart overcall but only if you can keep the numbers of undertricks to 2 or 3. With only 1 sure winner in your hand, making 9 tricks seems unlikely. Also, if you bid 3-hearts and the other side passes, you can be sure that they will not make an opening lead in Hearts. At this point it seems to makes no sense to do anything but pass.*

CHAPTER 6
QUIZ # 3, CONTINUED
THE SECOND SEAT REACTS TO OPENING BIDS

SCENARIO #6: FIRST SEAT OPENS 2-CLUBS.

        x x
        A Q 10 x x x
        x x x
        x x

Commentary # 11: You will overcall in 2-hearts, an overcall with preemptive values: This unbalanced shape has only 8VPs derived from 6HCPs+2LPs. While opener's artificial 2-club opening signals a powerful 22+VPs hand, your job as the Second Seat is to react to a 2-club opening bid be it conventional or natural. The only suit available in this hand that can legally overcall 2-clubs is Hearts at the 2-level. The guidance for making that overcall requires 5-11VPs and a good 6-card Heart suit. While it is unlikely that a weak-two overcall will be obstructive enough to prevent the other side from dominating the auction, you have done your bit in making it more difficult for them to do so. *Lessons Learned: As the defense you will want the opposition to bid high enough so that they will fail to make their contract. While you do not have many options to be seriously obstructive, you have done the best you can with what you have: you have also signaled your best suit for an opening lead. Finally, your overcall has made a 2-diamond waiting response by the Third Seat impossible.*

CHAPTER 7

THIRD SEAT RESPONDS TO A WIDE VARIETY OF OPENING BIDS

THE THIRD SEAT'S ROLE AND PRIORITIES

While the First Seat's priority is to open the bidding in Notrump, his partner's priority, in the Third Seat, is to identify at least an 8-card **FIT** in a major suit in their combined hand. This priority is based on observations showing that ***play in a major with an 8-card or longer fit will usually yield one or more tricks than play in Notrump, whether it is played in part-score or game***.

So, how does the side identify an 8-card fit in a major? The most usual method is via the 5-Card Major Bidding System where the First Seat opens in a major at the 1-level, promising at least a 5-card suit in a major. In that scenario, the Third Seat with 3-card Support, responds at the 2-level in the same major. With that response, the **GOLDEN FIT** of an 8-card major is identified.

Now, how is an 8-card fit in a major identified when the First Seat opens in Notrump at either the 1-level or the 2-level? To answer that question requires a familiarity with the defined Notrump balanced shapes.

NOTRUMP'S BALANCED SHAPES

FINDING 8-CARD FITS IN THE COMBINED HAND

Guidance only permits the three following shapes to be defined as Balanced for use in Notrump opening bids:

        5-3-3-2 (includes only one Short Suit, the Doubleton)
        4-3-3-3 (includes no Shortness)
        4-4-3-2 (includes only one Short suit, the Doubleton)

Beginner should note that there are no Singletons and no Voids in the three defined balanced shapes. Also, since there are only 4 different suit lengths within the 3 specified balanced hands (5-card, 4-card, 3-card, 2-card suits), there is a "good" chance that when the opening is in 1-notrump and responder holding a 5-card suit, the Notrump opener will have 3-card or more **SUPPORT,** in the same suit to insure at least an 8-card fit. However, the challenge is not to merely identify an 8-card fit in the same suit, but to identify an 8-card fit in a major suit. Why? Because, as stated above "play in a major with an 8-card or longer fit will usually yield one or more tricks than play in Notrump, whether it is played in part-score or game."

We start with the basic observation that the Notrump opener will hold one of the three defined balanced hands; and, the Notrump opening hand will hold two minor suits and two major suits. Based on that dynamic, the Responder's priority to a Notrump opening is to get the side to play in a major suit. In order to make that happen, the Third Seat uses Artificial bids which signal 4-card or 5-card or more holdings in a major suit.

Those Artificial bids are known as Stayman and Transfer Bids, respectively. Both of these Conventions will be discussed in detail further in this Chapter. Finally, if there is no 8-card match in a major, the Notrump opener's preferred alternative is to play in Notrump.

THE TRICK-TAKING MAGIC OF THE 8-CARD GOLDEN FIT

The guidance that pertains to playing in Notrump as opposed to play with an 8-card major suit fit is worth repeating: *play in a major suit with an 8-card fit (in the combined hand) will usually yield one or more tricks than play in Notrump whether it is played in part-score or game.*

With the above guidance in mind, let's try to understand why an 8-card fit has disproportionately more trick-taking power than a 7-card **IMPERFECT FIT:** when Declarers have 8 trump cards in their combined hand, the other side will have 5 trump cards in their combined hand. Declarer's 8-card suit will *most likely* Divide 5-3 and the other side's 5-card trump suit will *most likely* Divide 3-2. These two Divides are based on the Probability Table located at the end of this chapter. Of course, if there is Bidding Conversation information to the contrary, those Divides will take precedence over Probability Table Divides.

If the Declarers divide 5-3 and can win the first three tricks with their trumps, the other side is void in trumps by the end of the third trick (if beginner does not understand that sentence he is urged to re-read it since this is a fundamental strategy in the play of the tricks). After the third trick, the Declarers hold the 2 remaining trumps and there are no remaining cards the opponents can hold that can beat those 2 trumps. Also, with the other side void in trumps, the play is essentially in Notrump.

However, if the Declarers only have 7 trumps in their combined hand (an Imperfect Fit) the most trumps the other side can only have is 6 trumps; and, the most likely divides will be 4-3 for the Declarers and 4-2 for the other side. Now, in order to render the other side void of the trump suit, the Declarer will need to win 4 tricks to render them void of the trump suit; and, there will no trumps remaining with the Declarers that can be held in reserve. So, with a 7-card trump fit, the Declarers have two less trump tricks than they would if they had an 8-card trump fit. The difference between holding a 7-card fit and an 8-card fit, when both sides are in their most likely divides, is a disproportionate 2 extra tricks. And that's why the 8-card fit is called a **GOLDEN FIT.**

Any discussion of trick-taking and major suit fits inevitably leads to a discussion of trump cards and their ability to take tricks. For that reason, this is an appropriate time in the beginner's bridge journey to introduce the Law of Total Tricks and its impact on the bidding process.

THE LAW OF TOTAL TRICKS AND ITS LIMITS

THE LAW OF TOTAL TRICKS, a theory popularized by Larry Cohen, suggests that on any given deal *the total number of trumps in the combined hands of both sides* will approximate *the total number of tricks that can be made on that deal.* The "total number of tricks" is the sum of the number of tricks NS would take playing in their best fit and the number of tricks EW would take playing in their best fit. The OEB describes the Law as a "most useful bidding adjunct in competitive auctions."

The *"total number of trumps"* is defined as the sum of one side's longest trump fit of at least 7 cards and the other side's longest trump fit of at least 7 cards; totaling 14 tricks, in this Scenario. Obviously, this does not mean that, if both sides have 7 trumps that 14 tricks can be made by one side. What it does mean is that one side could make 8 tricks if the other side could only make 6 tricks. Also, if both sides have roughly equal points, both sides would likely be able to make 7 tricks.

The challenge for beginners, when applying the Law of Total Tricks, is determining the total number of trumps on each side. Declarers can work out, by deduction or other means, how many trumps each side has. For example, when Declarer holds the following hand, the Opening Bid, when playing 5-card Majors, is 1-heart, promising at least 5-card Hearts.

```
         A 8
         K Q 9 8 7
         A 9 2
         A 7 2
```

When the first Bidding Round goes like this, how should the opening bidder, South, holding 18VPs, ask partner to go to game in Hearts?

WEST	NORTH	EAST	SOUTH
			1-H
1-S	2-H	2-S	?

Based on this Bidding Conversation, we know that North identified at least an 8-card fit when he responded in 2-hearts, signaling 3-card Support for the Opening Bid. North also signals at least 6VPs. What we do not know is where South is within the 13-21VP range. We also do not know if South has more than a 5-card Heart suit.

Since South holds 18 VPs, he knows that the combined hand has at least 24 VPs and a game contract is likely. In that Scenario, South would not relinquish the Auction to NS; rather, he would invite game, asking partner to go to 4-hearts if he has more than 6-7VPs. How to invite partner to go to 4-hearts is a skill beyond the beginner level. However, if South rebids in 3-hearts, it could be because he holds a 6-card Heart suit and identifies a 9-card fit. So, to ensure that partner does not misunderstand the intent of South's rebid, he should make a **GAME TRY,** a bid in an unbid Side Suit that suggests interest in game and asks partner to reassess his values and make the final decision. Now, assuming that the Game Try bid was discussed in the Bidding Agreement Discussion, South could bid 3-clubs or 3-diamonds as a Game Try. Since Hearts have already been agreed upon by NS, there should be no confusion that partner is asking for more information.

If we change the Scenario slightly so that South only holds 13VPs, South now estimates the combined hand to have at least only 19VPs. South also knows that West's overcall signals at least a good 5-card Spade suit and that East's Advance in 2-spades signals at least 3-card support in Spades. South now knows EW likely have an 8-card Spade suit. At this point in the Auction, South must decide whether to raise the bidding to the 3-level in order to stay competitive, or to pass and allow EW to play in a Part-Score contract requiring 8 tricks.

Since both sides are likely relatively equal in terms of point-count strength, it appears that the Law of Total Tricks might be applicable in this Scenario. South calculates NS' longest trump fit to be at least an 8-card fit in Hearts and EW's longest trump fit to be at least an 8-card fit in Spades; 16 trumps in the combined hands of both sides. What that means is that neither side could make 9 tricks since both sides can only make 8 tricks. Of course, if NS could make 9 tricks and EW could only make 7 tricks, then the Law's formula would permit South to raise to the 3-level. Since NS can only make 8 tricks, South should pass.

THE LIMITS OF THE LAW OF TOTAL TRICKS

For beginning bridge players, The Law of Total Tricks is an especially good bidding guide for determining "how high" a side should go in the bidding; the *OEB* indicates that a "simple way to use the Law is to usually bid to the level of your side's number of trumps in competitive Auctions." For example, compete to the 2-level with 8 trumps, the 3-level with 9 trumps, and the 4-level with 10 trumps.

At the same time, it is important for the beginner to recognize that the number of trumps in a combined hand will not always generate that same number of tricks. The accuracy of the Law's formula may be affected by such factors as extreme distribution, possession of Queens and Jacks in the opponents' suits and double fits.

An extreme example in which the Law of Total Tricks would not apply would be when both sides have an 8-card fit and one side has almost all of the HCPs. For example, when a side with an 8-card fit holds 37HCPs and the other side, also with an 8-card fit holds 3HCPs, the side with the 37HCPs should bid 13 tricks since his point-count renders the Law is inapplicable in that situation. In the end, using the Law of Total Tricks, even with its limitations, is a beginner skill; and, an excellent guideline that permits the beginner to bid to the level of his side's number of trumps.

More importantly, making the bid based on the Law of Total Tricks and failing may frequently be better than letting the opponents take the bid. It may also help you push the other side beyond what they could make. Finally, the discussion on the Law of Total Tricks is an excellent teaching device since it covers many of the skills needed in beginning bridge: listening to the Bidding Conversations; deducing the enemy's suit lengths, likely Divide probabilities; and, an understanding of the relative differences between point-counts and trump card fits.

As promised, we now return to the subject of Notrump openings and the Responder's priority to get the side to play in a major suit.

RESPONDING TO NOTRUMP OPENINGS

WITH A 5-CARD MAJOR, USING A TRANSFER BID

In the following scenario we will examine a bidding sequence in which the responder to a 1-notrump opening, holding at least a 5-card suit, responds with a **TRANSFER BID,** an Artificial bid showing rank of suit immediately below the actual suit held.

SCENARIO: Notrump opener holds 15HCPs in a balanced 4-4-3-2 shape where the Short suit is a Doubleton in Hearts. Responder holds 11VPs and a 5-card suit in Hearts. Of course, Responder is not aware that the opener's Hearts are a Doubleton. This is what the bidding looks like when the Transfer Bid is incorporated into the beginner's skill set:

Round # 1   1-notrump---pass---2-diamonds---pass
Round # 2   2-hearts---pass---3-notrump---pass
Round # 3   pass---pass

The bidding begins in Round # 1 with a standard 1-Notrump opening followed by a pass; and, then Responder's 2-diamond Transfer Bid signaling a 5-card or more Heart suit (according to the Transfer Convention, responses in Diamonds signal Hearts and responses in Hearts signal Spades). The Transfer provides no Signal regarding Responder's strength.

In Round # 2, Opener accepts the Transfer by rebidding in 2-hearts, making him the Declarer and ensuring that the side's stronger hand remains hidden if the game is played in Hearts. The Opener has no choice since the Convention, to be effective, requires that the Transfer is accepted by the Opener, regardless of the number of Hearts he may or may not hold. However, if the Notrump opener has 17HCPS, the top of his point-count range and a 4-card Heart suit he can take the transfer in 3-hearts, a highly Invitational Bid rather than the 2-heart transfer.

Also, in Round # 2, having already described his 5-card or more Hearts, it is now Responder's first opportunity to describe his actual strength to the Opener. As indicated in the Scenario, Responder holds 11VPs, an intermediate hand. Responder's estimate for the strength in the combined hand is 26VPs (at least 15 in the opener and 11 known in his hand); since there is enough strength in the combined hand for a game bid in Notrump, the responder's rebid is 3-notrump. Despite this rebid, Responder's priority remains to play in an 8-card major suit fit in Hearts if possible.

Now in Round # 3, it is opener's first opportunity to signal the number of Hearts he holds in his balanced 4-4-3-2 hand. As the Scenario indicates, the 2-card suit in the Notrump opener's hand is in Hearts; and, as a result, there is no 3-card or more Support that would identify at least an 8-card suit in a major. Why is that important? Let's repeat the guidance for this situation: *play in a major suit with an 8-card or longer fit will usually yield one or more tricks that play in Notrump whether it is played in part-score or game.*

Since the side is already at the 3-notrump level, the cheapest legal level available for play in Hearts would be a 4-level game bid in Hearts, requiring 10 tricks. Since that would require playing a game bid in a major suit with an Imperfect Fit (less than 8-card) in Hearts; the best decision for the opener, especially since he identifies at least 26VPs in the combined hand is to pass and play in 3-notrump, a game contract that only requires 9 tricks.

While Transfer Bidding pushes the envelope of beginning bridge, having a skill that identifies an 8-card or more fit; avoids the cursed 7-card Imperfect Fit; and, keeps the stronger hand hidden, is well worth the effort. Now, when an advanced player asks if you "do **JACOBY**," the inventor of the Transfer Bid, you can proudly acknowledge this accomplishment!

WITH A 4-CARD MAJOR: THE 2-CLUB STAYMAN

The Transfer bid cannot be made when Responder to a Notrump opening only holds a 4-card major. Nevertheless, the priority to play in a major with an 8-card fit remains in effect. When holding a 4-card major, Responder still has a "good" chance to identify an 8-card fit in his combined hand. The bridge skill that makes it possible to explore that possibility is the **STAYMAN** Convention discussed below:

Responder's priority to a 1-notrump opening, with one or two 4-card majors, is to identify an 8-card major suit fit in the combined hand. The Responder's challenge is to determine if the Notrump opener has a 4-card suit in the same 4-card major suit that he holds. Here's how the Stayman works: following a 1-notrump opening, Responder, with 8+HCPs, makes a 2-club Artificial bid, signaling at least one 4-card major. This Convention is so universally known that there is no need to announce "**ALERT.**" The first round of bidding looks like this:

Round #1: 1-notrump---pass---2-clubs---pass

Not all Stayman responses are in 2-clubs. For example, in the following bidding sequence, the opening is a Weak-Two; the Overcall is in 2-notrump; and, with the Fourth Seat holding a 4-card major, the 3-club Advance is used as the Stayman convention to identify a 4—4 major suit match in the combined hands of the Second Seat and the Fourth Seat. The bidding could look like this:

Round #1: 2-spades---2-notrump---pass---3-clubs

Beginner should ensure that the 3-club advance is part of the bidding agreement.

THE BIDDING "CONVERSATION" FOLLOWING A 2-CLUB STAYMAN RESPONSE TO 1-NOTRUMP

Whether a Stayman follows a Notrump opening bid by the First Seat or a Notrump overcall by the Second Seat, the Bidding Conversation that the 1-notrump opener initiates following the Stayman response includes one of the three possible rebids opener can make:

1. Opener has no 4-card major

2. Opener has two 4-card majors

3. Opener only has one 4-card major

The following describes the bidding in each of the above 3 possible response Scenarios:

SCENARIO: This basic Scenario remains constant in all the following possible rebids by the Notrump opener: Notrump opener has 15HCPs in a balanced hand; and, Responder with 9HCPs and a 4-card Heart suit responds with the 2-club Stayman. Now, let's "listen" to the three possible rebids by the Notrump opener in the following sub-scenarios:

- **2-diamonds,** a Conventional rebid by the Notrump opener signaling that no 4-card major is available. The Bidding Sequence looks like this:

    Round # 1:   1-notrump---pass---2-clubs---pass

In Round # 1, above, following a 1-notrump opening bid, Responder with at least 8 HCPs, signals that he holds at least one 4-card suit in a major and is looking for a 4—4 match in the combined hand.

    Round # 2:   2-diamonds---pass---2-notrump---pass

In Round # 2: the opener's rebid of 2-diamonds is the Convention signaling that he does not hold a 4-card suit in any major. Opener now estimates the combined hand to have 23VPs (15HCPs known in his hand from the Scenario and at least 8HCPs in the Responder). The Responder's priority is now to play in Notrump; and, his 2-notrump rebid signals an **INVITATIONAL HAND,** one with 8-9HCPs. Note, the Responder does not need a balanced hand to respond in Notrump to a Notrump opening.

    Round # 3:   pass---pass

In Round # 3, Opener passes since he estimates the combined hand to have not enough for game in Notrump (15HCPs known and at least 8 in Responder).

- **2-hearts,** a Conventional rebid by the Opener signaling a 4-card Heart suit "while not denying a 4-card Spade suit;" "Bridge-Speak" meaning opener may hold four Hearts and 4 Spades and is **BIDDING UP THE LINE,** starting with Hearts. Since both Responder and Opener, in this sub-scenario have 4-card Heart suits, a 4—4 major suit match is made and an 8-card fit in Hearts is identified.

    Round # 1:   1-notrump---pass---2-clubs---pass

In Round # 1, the bidding is exactly the same as the Round # 1 of the first Scenario.

    Round # 2:   2-hearts---pass---3-hearts---pass

In Round # 2, opener signals the availability of at least a 4-card Heart suit; while not denying a 4-card Spade suit. The Stayman Convention requires that, with two 4+Card major suits available, the opener bids "up the line" starting with Hearts. Accordingly, a 2-heart rebid is made by the opener. The basic Scenario indicates that responder has only one 4-card suit, which happens to be in Hearts. Having now identified a 4—4 major suit match in Hearts in the combined hand, Responder now estimates the combined hand may or may not have enough for game in a major (at least 15HCPs in opener and 9HCPs known in responder); and, accordingly, rebids 3-hearts, with an **INVITATIONAL HAND.**

    Round # 3   pass---pass

In Round # 3, it is now the opener's turn to estimate the combined hand's strength. Since at least 8HCPs are required for a Stayman, opener, with 15HCPs, also estimates the combined hand to only have 23VPs, not enough strength to go to game. The final bid is 3-hearts, a Part-Score contract requiring 9 tricks

- **2-spades,** a Conventional rebid by the opener, signaling only a 4-card major suit, Spades. Since the Responder, in the basic Scenario only holds a 4-card major in Hearts, a 4—4 match in Spades is not possible. The first round of bidding is the same in all Scenarios

    Round # 1:   1-notrump---pass---2-clubs---pass

    Round # 2:   2-spades---pass---2-notrump---pass

In the second round, after learning that a 4—4 match in a major is not possible, Responder holding 9HCPs defaults to his second priority and rebids 2-notrump.

    Round # 3:   pass--- pass

In Round # 3, Opener estimates the combined hand to have only 23VPs (15HCPs in opener and at least 8HCPs in responder), not enough for a game bid in Notrump and passes. The final contract is in 2-notrump, a part-score requiring 8 tricks.

Beginner should note that, in all of the three bidding sequences shown above, the Responder, according to the Scenario had 9VPs, an **INVITATIONAL HAND.** With 10+VPs, the Responder's hand would have been considered **GAME-GOING,** especially with the opener holding 15HCPs in this Scenario.

RESPONDING IN NOTRUMP

When neither the Transfer nor the Stayman are available, two options remain if Responder wants to compete: play in Notrump; or, play in a minor, in that order. Since the Opening is in Notrump, a balanced hand is not needed to respond in Notrump since the side already has one hand Suitable for Notrump.. The following responses in Notrump to a Notrump opening bid is based on the following strength levels in the responder:

BIDDING UP TO 3-NOTRUMP

- 0-7VPs pass. The side has 15HCPs at the least and belongs in a partscore contract at the 1-level.

- 8-9VPs, an **INVITATIONAL HAND,** raise the opening to 2-notrump, a response which does not force partnership to game. The side has at least 23VPs and if opener is at the top of his 15-17HCP range, he may accept the invitation and go to game.

- 10-15VPs go to 3-notrump, a Game Bid.

NO BIDDING BEYOND 3-NOTRUMP---A TUTORIAL ON RUBBER-SCORING

- 16-17VPs, do not bid above 3-notrump. When responding to a 1-notrump opening bid, there is no need to bid any more than 3-notrump even though the combined hand has at least 31VPs. Whether 9 tricks are made or bid-and-made, the side earns **100** Trick-Score Points (TSPs) scored for the 3 tricks made above the first 6 tricks in Book, derived as follows: 40 TSPs for the first trick over book in Notrump plus 30 TSPS for each of the two additional tricks made over book. There are no bonus points for making the first game or the second game in a Rubber. However, a Rubber Bonus is earned by the first side to win 2 games of the 3 game Rubber. The size of the Rubber Bonus depends on whether the Rubber was won 2-0 or 2-1, with 2-0 earning the larger bonus. If the same 3-notrump contract was bid and the side made 10 tricks, the Total Point-Score would be **130 TSPs** derived as follows: 40 TSPs for the first Notrump trick made over book and 30 TSPs each for the next 3 tricks.

Since game in Notrump only requires 100 TSPs, the first 3 tricks over book are applied to the game requirement; and, the remaining tricks, in excess of the contract's requirement are Overtricks, scored above-the-line, not applied to game. ***However, if you bid 4-notrump and make only 9 tricks***, *you go down one trick. This one trick less than what is required by the contract is known as an Undertrick.* In that scenario, even though your side takes 9 tricks, it scores ZERO TSPs and the other side is awarded Penalty Points, based on whether your contract was doubled or undoubled and your side was vulnerable or non-vulnerable.

As shown above, in a Rubber Scoring Format, your **TOTAL POINT-SCORE,** the sum of all points earned from Scoring Events is based on the number of tricks MADE not BID. So, why would you bid 4-notrump, promising 10 tricks and risk not making your contract, to make the same TSPs if you BID 3-notrump, promising 9 tricks and make 10 tricks? The only exception is the Slam Bonus which must be BID and Made.

The Rubber Bonus is earned by the first side to win 2 games in a Rubber. The size of the Rubber Bonus depends on whether you win 2-0 or 2-1. Note you win games by scoring 100 or more TSPs. For example, you make game if you make 9 tricks in Notrump; 10 tricks in a major suit game contract; or if you make 11 tricks in a minor suit game contract. In any one of those successful game contracts you will earn 100 or more TSPs. When you make a series of part-score contracts, whose individual scores add up to 100TSPs or more, you can also score a game.

- 18+VPs, do not bid above 3-notrump. Combined hand has at least 33VPs, enough for a Small Slam, requiring 12 of the 13 tricks in the play. In addition to the raw power of points, you will also need Slam Bidding skills to play in a difficult contract that allows the Defense to defeat your contract with only 2 tricks. Why? Because if your side's combined hand has two Aces, that means the Defense also has two Aces as well as the advantage of making the opening lead. If play is in Notrump and the two Aces take the first two tricks, your Small Slam Bid is toast! Slam bidding skills would help you identify where the Aces are before you make a Slam bid.

- If your side holds 33HCPs, you do not need Slam Bidding skills to know the other side cannot hold 2 Aces (8HCPs) since that would exceed the 40HCPs, the maximum number available in a combined hand. However, with 33HCPs and 3 Aces you still can be in danger since the other side could have the A K (7HCPs) and still take two quick tricks which would quickly dash your side's hopes for a successful Small Slam bid. For that reason Slam Bidding is one of the first skills you will want to acquire after completing your beginning bridge journey.

In summary, there is no need for beginners without Slam bidding skills to bid beyond 3-notrump. See Chapter 11 for a more robust discussion of the Rubber Scoring Format.

RESPONDING TO OPENINGS IN A MAJOR SUIT

WITH 3-CARD OR MORE SUPPORT

When an opening bid in Notrump is not available, the First Seat's next priority is to open with a 5-card or longer major suit and 13-21VPs. The priority of the opener's partner, the Responder, is to Support or Raise the major suit opening with at least a 3-card suit of the opening suit bid. To **RAISE** means that opener's partner makes a bid increasing the level of the strain named by his partner, the Opener..

A Raise to the 2-level, signals 6-10VPs in the Responder and identifies at least an 8-card major suit fit if the combined hand. The following is the guidance for the Responder with 3-card or more Support for the opening bid in a major suit:

- With 0-5 VPs pass since, even with 3-card support and an 8-card major suit fit, game is unlikely. Contract is best played in the major suit in part-score at the 1-level. However, with 5-card support at least a 10-card fit is identified and a Preemptive Jump Raise to game at the 4-level is permitted by the Law of Total Tricks. Opener will recognize that Responder's Jump Bid is made on the basis of trumps in the combined hand and not on the basis of a point-count.

- With 6-10 VPs, and 3-card support, the opening bid is Raised to the 2-level, identifying at least an 8-card major suit fit and at least 19 VPs in the combined hand. With only 6-9 VPs and 4-card Support, Raise to the 2-level. If the opponents do not let you rest at the 8 trick level, you will be willing to get pushed to the 9 trick level since you have 9 trumps. With 10-11VPs and 4-card support, you indicate that strength and length by making a "limit raise" to the 3-level, inviting partner to go to game if he has just a little more than a minimum opener. Responder, as the likely dummy, can revalue the hand with Dummy Points for Shortness in lieu of Length Points. Again, with 5-card support at least a 10-card major suit fit is identified and, Responder can make a 4-level Game Bid based on the Law of Total Tricks. This is a strategic bid and may fail to make. The essence of the Law is that it may be better to make the bid and go down than letting the opponents take the bid. Further, following the bidding levels suggested by this theory may push the other side to bid higher than they normally would have bid.

- With 11-12 VPs the combined hand has at least 24 VPs and a **GAME-GOING** bid or Part-Score is in sight. With only 3-card support, Responder should bid a 4-card or longer New Suit at the cheapest level, a forcing bid; and, then, at the next opportunity to bid, Support partner's major suit opening at the 3-level, signaling 11-12 VPs and only 3-card support. With 4-card support, the guidance is to Jump Raise the opening bid to the 3-level, an invitational bid signaling Intermediate Strength and more than 3-card support. Opener, knowing that responder has at least 11 VPs, will go to game with a little more than Minimum Opening Strength (13-16VPs).

- With 13-15 VPs and at least 3-card Support, at least an 8-card fit is identified and the combined hand has at least 26 VPs. The guidance is to get to game by bidding a New 4-card or longer suit at the cheapest level and Jumping to game at the 4-level at the next opportunity to bid.

- With 16+VPs, and at least 3-card support there is no need to respond beyond the 4-level in a major since a side that bids 4-(10 tricks) and makes 5 (11 tricks) makes the same Total Point-Score as a side that bids 5 (11 tricks) and makes 5 (11 tricks). Both bids make game in a Rubber and both earn a Total Point-Score of 150. See Chapter 11 for a more robust discussion on scoring in a Rubber Scoring Format.

WITH NO SUPPORT IN THE OTHER MAJOR AS A NEW SUIT

When Responding to an Opening in a major suit, the priority is to always provide Support; the second priority, when there is no Support, is to introduce the other major as a **NEW SUIT,** an unbid suit in the Auction. For example, if the Opening Bid is in 1-heart, Responder, without support, can introduce a 4-card or longer Spade suit at the 1-level with 6+VPs as the New Suit. However, if Opening is in 1-spade, Responder, without Support, can introduce at the 2-level with 11+VPs a 5-card or longer Heart suit as a New Suit; or, with 11+ VPs and a 4-card or longer minor suit, that suit can be introduced as a New Suit Note that New Suit responses are always forcing. Let's look at a hand, with 6-10VPs, that can introduce Spades as a New Suit when the opening is in 1-heart:

> K 9 5 4 3
> 5 3
> Q 9 8
> A 10 6

With 6 or more VPs and a 4-card or longer Spade suit, Spades can be introduced at the 1-level. The combined hand is estimated by Responder to hold at least 23 VPs (at least 13 in opener and 10 known in responder While this Balanced Hand could also be introduced in 1-notrump, the priority is to play in a major ahead of play in Notrump. Opener will know that Responder has at least a 4-card Spade suit and if he holds a 4-card Spade suit, there is a possibility that a 4—4 Spade match can be identified in the combined hand.

RESPONDING IN NOTRUMP

Without support for the opening in a major; and not enough strength to introduce a New Suit (major or minor) at the 1-level or 2-level, the only alternative left is to respond in 1-notrump with a hand that may or may not be Suitable for Play in Notrump. Such a hand with 6-10VPs would be the following *when the opening is in 1-heart:*

> J 9 2
> 5
> K 8 7 5 4 2
> A 6 5

Since the Heart suit is a Singleton, there is no Support for the opening in Hearts; the 3-card Spade suit cannot be introduced as a New Suit at the 1-level because that requires a 4-card or longer Spade suit; and, neither of the two minor suits can be introduced as New Suits since that would require a 2-level bid and 11+VPs and this hand only holds 10 VPs derived from 8 HCPs+2LPs from the 6-card Diamonds. While this hand is unbalanced, the 1-notrump Response to the opening in a major suit *does not require a balanced hand, it clearly signals that no other options are available and the hand only has 6-10 VPs.*

RESPONDING IN A MINOR SUIT

The opening is in 1-spade; and, a response in a minor suit is recommended ahead of a Notrump response.

> K 4
> 5 3 2
> K J 9 6 5 4
> Q 10

Responder, with 11VPs derived from 9 HCPs+2LPs, has no 3-card support for the opening in Spades; and, is unable to introduce the other major, Hearts, as a New Suit because it requires a 5-card Heart suit. With Hearts unavailable, play in a major suit is not possible. Since minor suits are not a priority, Responder investigates playing in Notrump but determines that the Hand is unsuitable since it is unbalanced.

While play in a minor is more risky than any other alternative, this hand has at least 24 VPs in the combined hand. Accordingly, with a 4-card or longer minor suit and 11+VPs the guidance is to respond in a minor suit at the 2-level. Since Diamonds are the ranking and longer minor suit, the guidance is to respond in 2-diamonds, requiring 8 tricks. Since the minor suit response is the only alternative, it is clearly a better alternative than a pass. How high this bidding will go depends on where the opener is within his 13-21VP range.

OPENINGS IN A MINOR SUIT

When the First Seat has Opening Strength but cannot meet the guidance for an opening in a major or in Notrump, the only option left is an opening bid in a minor suit. While openings in a minor are the last priority because they entail a higher risk, they are not infrequent. Minor suit openings require 13-21VPs; at least a 3-card minor suit as the "Best Minor;" and, should never be opened in a Doubleton minor suit. Actually, a minor suit opening is more likely to be opened with a 4-card or longer suit.

RESPONDING WITH A MAJOR SUIT

The first priority for the responder to a minor suit opening is to introduce a major suit at the 1-level as a New Suit, a forcing alternative. The guidance requires 6+VPs and a 4-card or longer major suit. In that scenario, the combined hand could only have at least 19VPs.and the bidding would look like this when the major is in Spades:

Round # 1:   1-club---pass---1-spade---pass

RESPONDING WITH A JUMP SHIFT

With 17+VPs and a 5+suit in Spades, Responder to a minor suit opening can introduce Spades as a New suit at the 2-level. This response is known as a **JUMP SHIFT** when the response is in a New Suit at the 2-level. The combined hand now is estimated to hold at least 30VPs and the opener is forced to keep the bidding alive until game has been reached. Responder's priorities are, of course to identify at least an 8-card fit with a game contract in a major.

Because Slam bidding skills are not part of Beginning Bridge, bidding in a major suit game contract is capped at the 4-level, requiring 10 tricks. Of course, with 30 VPs or more, more than 10 tricks are possible and the side will earn a score based on the rules of the Rubber Scoring format. What they will not earn is a Slam Bonus. A Jump Shift bid would look like in Round #1 this when the 5-card major is in Spades and like this in Round # 2, when Opener with 3-card Support for Spades goes to game.

Round # 1:   1-club---pass---2-spades—pass
Round #2:   4-spades---pass---pass---pass

RESPONDING IN NOTRUMP

When Response in a major to a minor suit opening is not possible, the second priority, *even with Support for the opening minor suit bid, is to consider a Notrump contract ahead of a minor suit contract; game in Notrump requires only 9 tricks while game in a minor requires 11 tricks; and, part-score contracts in Notrump yield more trick-score points than the same part-score contract in a minor suit.* With no 4-card major suit and a balanced hand, Suitable for Notrump, the guidance is to make a non-forcing response in Notrump based on the following strength levels held by the responder:

- 6-10VPs, respond 1-notrump
- 11-12VPs, respond 2-notrump
- 13-15VPs, respond 3-notrump

By bidding some number of Notrump as a response to a minor suit opening, you are denying a 4-card major since that is your priority if you had a major to bid.

When responding in Notrump to a minor suit opening, a Suitable hand for Notrump is required, including a balanced hand and Stoppers in at least 3 suits, especially those in the suits bid or held by the other side. Beginner should chance 3-notrump, game with 13+VPs rather than settle for a part-score contract in a minor suit. It is worth repeating that, even with support for the minor suit opening, the guidance is to play in Notrump. According to the OEB, more game contracts are played at Notrump than in any other denomination.

RAISE OPENER'S MINOR SUIT

Without a major suit fit and a hand Not Suitable for Notrump, the last priority is to find an 8-card or longer fit in the Opening Bidder's minor suit bid. Beginners should usually consider the term "Unsuitable for Notrump" to mean an unbalanced hand or a balanced hand with Stoppers in less than three of the suits.

While a minor suit opening can be made with only a 3-card minor, it is more likely that the opener will have a 4-card or longer suit. Accordingly, the guidance permits Responder to identify an 8-card minor suit fit when Raising a minor suit opening with 4-card or longer support and holding the following strength levels:

- 6-10VPs, raise to the 2-level
- 11-12VPs, raise to the 3-level
- 13+VPs, get to the game level

Note, since minor suit contracts need 28-29VPs, beginning guidance does not recommend making a Jump from the 3-level to the 5-level unless Responder's hand is very unbalanced. Instead, it may be more effective to go to the 4-level in the minor suit, inviting the opener to go to game. Obviously, with a Suitable Hand and since the combined hand has at least 26VPs, it may be more appropriate to go to game in 3-notrump.

COUNTING DUMMY POINTS WHEN RAISING OPENER'S MINOR SUIT

Unlike raising a major suit opening, when raising opener's minor suit, guidance permits Responder to identify a fit with 4-card or longer Support. As the likely dummy, Responder can revalue for Shortness in lieu of Length Points. In that Scenario, playing in a minor suit and holding Short Suits may be an asset. However, if the Scenario changes and the final contract is Notrump, Shortness is no longer an asset. So what's a beginner to do? The guidance suggests that Dummy Points not be counted unless there is no chance that the hand will be played in Notrump. For example, when holding a very unbalanced hand and the long suit in a minor, play in Notrump is highly unlikely.

RESPONDING TO 3-LEVEL AND 4-LEVEL PREEMPTIVE OPENING BIDS

One of the main advantages of Preemptive Openings is that they are very descriptive: holding good 6-card, 7-card or 8-card suits; and, with less than opening strength they may make the other side bid higher than they would if the opening was at the 1-level. For example, the 3-level Preemptive Opening Bid, signals a good 7-card suit; 5 or 6 playing tricks if the Hand is played in the Opening Suit bid; and, less than opening strength. In that Scenario, Responder is more concerned with Sure Winners than with point-counts. Responder has 3 options: Raise the 3-level Opening with Support; bid Notrump, or pass. Because the Preemptive opening signals less than opening strength, the guidance for Responder, with less than 3-card support is to pass.

With 3-card support for a 3-level preemptive opening in a major, the Responder identifies a 10-card fit and goes to game at the 4-level. While the Law of Total Tricks may support the game bid, it is possible that the required 10 tricks will not be made since the majority of the strength is likely with the other side. However, failing to make the 4-level contract may still be better than letting the opponents make their sure game or even Slam. This is the essence of the Law of Total Tricks.

Of course, if the 3-level Preemptive Opening is in a minor, the Responder may have a good 6-card or longer major suit and can introduce it as a New Suit. Finally, responding in Notrump is the least likely option that may be available.

WHEN THE OPENING IS AT THE 2-LEVEL—THE WEAK-TWO

The 2-level opening suit bid, while known as a Weak-Two bid is also preemptive, showing a good 6-card suit and only 5-11VPs, less than Opening Strength. If your bidding agreement includes the 2-club strong, artificial opening, a weak-two can be made in any suit except Clubs. The tactical advantage of a Weak-Two opening is that, with a weak hand, it has the potential to make the other side bid higher than they would if the opening was at the 1-level. Another advantage is that the weak-two, like the 3-level and 4-level preemptive opening bids is very descriptive. Responder, with 3-card Support can identify 9 trump cards in the combined hand and consider a raise to the 3-level, making it difficult for the opponents to find a game or a Slam. This raise is non-forcing and again is an illustration of the Law of Total Tricks.

RESPONDING TO STRONG 2-CLUB ARTFICIAL OPENING BIDS

The guidance for responding to the **STRONG 2-CLUB ARTIFICIAL OPENING BID**, is to make a **POSITIVE RESPONSE** when holding a good 5-card major suit and 8+VPs. When that response is not available, the guidance is to make the **2-DIAMOND WAITING BID** which permits Responder to see what the Opener's rebid will be. If the rebid is in 2-notrump, signaling 22-24VPs and if partner can bid the Stayman or Transfer, the bidding is more effective since it permits the stronger hand to be the Declarer. At the same time, if the hand belongs in Notrump, the stronger hand is with the Declarer.

If partner, with 8+VPs and a balanced hand had responded in 2-notrump and the final contract was in Notrump, the significantly stronger hand would have been the visible dummy,

WHEN THIRD SEAT FOLLOWS A SUIT OVERCALL,

The Third Seat frequently finds himself in a competitive Auction in which partner's Opening suit bid is challenged by a suit Overcall. At that point, the Auction becomes competitive and Responder's options are different than when the Auction is non-competitive. For example, Responder in the Third Seat can follow a suit Overcall from the Second Seat by bidding a Double for Takeout, known as a **NEGATIVE DOUBLE** which is likely to hold only 2 unbid suits.

The Negative Double requires less than opening strength; and, depends on the level in which the opener will be forced to make his rebid. For example, when opening is in 1-spade and the overcall is in 2-diamonds, responder has two 4-card unbid suits, Hearts and Clubs. If opener selects Hearts as trump and needs to bid at the 2-level to be legal, the Negative Doubler would only need to hold 6 or more points; if the opener would have to rebid at the 3-level, negative doubler needs 9+VPs; and, if at the 4-level, 11+VPs would be needed.

RESPONDING AFTER PARTNER OPENS IN 7-NOTRUMP, A GRAND SLAM

A **PERFECT BRIDGE HAND** is defined in the OEB as a hand that will produce 13 tricks in Notrump irrespective of the Opening Lead or the composition of the other three hands. While this is a very rare occasion, it is not all that rare: actually there 3,756 possible perfect bridge hands and the possibility of getting one is only 169 million to 1. So, what's a beginner as the Responder in the Third Seat to do when the opening is in 7-notrump? ENJOY! Your partner, who is obviously no beginner, knows what to do when dealt a perfect bridge hand: contain one's emotions and open the bidding in 7-notrump. Your job as responder is to simply pass and watch partner collect his 13 tricks.

Actually, other than the Pass there is no legal response you can make since 7-Notrump is the highest bid in the ladder. Here is what the most common perfect bridge hand looks like:

A K Q J x x x x x
A K
A
A

It is interesting to note that this hand holds 30 VPs derived from 25 HCPs and 5 LPs, not enough for bidding a Small Slam. However, if you are counting Sure Winners, the hand has 9 in Spades; 2 in Hearts; 1 in Diamonds; and, 1 in Clubs; that is 13 tricks, just enough for a Grand Slam. A hand containing all 13 cards of a suit, will not qualify as a Perfect Bridge Hand since it will not take even a single trick if played in Notrump.

CHAPTER 7
FIGURE # 2

PROBABILITY TABLES ON HOW SUIT LENGTHS DIVIDE IN A COMBINED HAND

SUIT LENGTH	DIVIDES	PERCENT
1	1-0	100
2	1-1	52
	2-0	48
3	2-1	78
	3-0	22
4	3-1	50
	2-2	40
	4-0	10
5	3-2	68
	4-1	28
	5-0	4
6	4-2	48
	3-3	35
	5-1	15
	6-0	2
7	4-3	62
	5-2	31
	6-1	6
	7-0	1
8	5-3	47
	4-4	33
	6-2	17
	7-1	2
	8-0	1

A **DIVIDE** is a bridge term which indicates the ways in which suit lengths in terms of numbers of cards in a suit can be fractionated. For example, the 5-card suit is divided into three combinations of divides: 3-2; 4-1; and, 5-0 and the likelihood of each one of those occurring are 68%; 28%; and 4% respectively. So, one can say that the most likely divide for a 5-card suit is 3-2 with a 68% probability.

If you as declarer are holding the AKQJ10 of a suit and the dummy holds the 987 of the same suit, you can deduce that opponents hold the 65432 in their combined hand. This Table tells you that the 65432 will likely divide 3-2, 68% of the time. What the Table cannot tell you is which of the 2 hands in the defense hold the 3-card suit and which hold the 2-card suit. It also cannot tell you how the 65432 cards are distributed within the 2 divides.

CHAPTER 7
QUIZ # 4
THIRD SEAT RESPONDS TO A VARIETY OF OPENING BIDS

SCENARIO # 1: OPENING BID IS 1-NOTRUMP, SECOND SEAT PASSES, YOUR RESPONSE AS THIRD SEAT WITH THE FOLLOWING HANDS?

J 10 9 x
J 10
K 10 9x
Q J 9

Commentary # 1: You respond in 2-clubs, Stayman: This balanced 4-4-3-2 shape's initial point-count of 8 HCPs has the minimum required for a 2-club Stayman artificial response to an opening in 1-Notrump. Third Seat's priority, when responding to a 1-notrump opening is to identify at least an 8-card major suit fit in the combined hand. Responder estimates the combined hand's point-count to be at least 23VPs, close to game. With a 4-card Spade suit and 8HCPs, your only option for identifying an 8-card or longer major suit fit is the Stayman. *Lessons Learned: While you always want your partner to open in Notrump, as responder, you always want your side to play in a major. The Stayman makes possible the identifying of a 4—4 major suit fit. The Stayman is so well known that the responder does not need to execute the "ALERT" protocol. If opener has no 4-card support in either major, he makes a conventional bid in 2-diamonds, signaling play in any major is not available; and, you will respond in 2-notrump, an Invitational bid. At his next opportunity to bid, if opener is at the top of his range, he will rebid 3-notrump, game. It is not necessary to hold a hand suitable for play in Notrump when responding in Notrump. Stated another way, a response in Notrump does not require a balanced hand, only an opening in Notrump requires a balanced hand.*

x x
A K Q x x
x x x
x x x

Commentary # 2: You respond in 2-diamonds, a Transfer bid. A 5-card suit in Hearts is all that is needed to response to a 1-notrump opening with the 2-diamond Transfer bid, one suit level below the actual major suit held. The convention usually requires the opener to take the Transfer with a 2-heart rebid; establishing himself as the Declarer as well as keeping the stronger hand hidden. However, if opener is at the top of his range (17HCPs) with a 4-card Heart suit, he identifies a 9-card fit in Hearts and can take the transfer in 3-hearts, a highly Invitational bid. Based on that scenario, Responder with 10 VPs will estimate the combined hand to hold at least 27VPs, enough for game and rebids 4-hearts, promising 10 tricks. *Lessons Learned: With the Transfer taken at the 2-level, Responder estimates at least 25VPs in the combined hand and would rebid 3-notrump after opener takes the transfer. Opener with only 2 Hearts will pass since an 8-card fit in Hearts may not be likely; but, with 3 Hearts, opener identifies an 8-card fit and will go to 4-hearts, game.*

CHAPTER 7
QUIZ # 4 CONTINUED
THIRD SEAT RESPONDS TO A VARIETY OF OPENING BIDS

SCENARIO # 1 CONTINUED

```
x x
K J
K x x x
A 10 x x x
```

Commentary # 3: Your response to the 1-notrump opening is 3-notrump. Your response is a game bid in Notrump, promising 9 tricks. This unbalanced 5-4-2-2 shape has 12VPs derived from 11 HCPs+1LPs. The combined hand has at least 27 VPs, more than enough for game in Notrump. The role of the Responder in Notrump is to determine "how high" and "where" the bidding should go. With this combined hand's point-count, responder answers the how high question. Without at least a 5-card or a 4-card major suit, neither a Transfer nor a Stayman bid is available. The correct answer to the "where" question is Notrump which does not require a balanced hand to respond to an opening in Notrump. *Lesson learned: Exploring the possibility of a Game bid in a minor makes no sense when Responder estimates the combined hand to have enough strength for a Game bid in Notrump; and game needs only 9 tricks while yielding the same number of trick-score points (100) as a game contract in a minor, requiring 11 tricks. Also, the stronger hand remains hidden when playing in Notrump.*

SCENARIO # 2: OPENING 1-SPADE, OVERCALL 2-HEARTS, YOUR RESPONSE AS THIRD SEAT?

```
x x x x
Void
Q x x x
x x x x x
```

Commentary # 4: You raise the opening bid to 3–spades: With 4-card support and a weak hand, your response is a preemptive jump intending to interfere with the other side's bidding. Since this bid is 1-level higher than necessary, opener should have no problem interpreting your raise, signaling 4-card support and 6-9 VPs. Since you are now the likely Dummy you add 5DPs for the Void in Hearts exclude LPs and settle for a final point-count of 8VPs, a weak hand. Responder now estimates the combined hand to have at least 21 VPs (at least 13 VPs in the opener and 8 known in his hand), not enough for game. In order for the other side to remain competitive, the advance must be in at least 3-notrump. If the fourth Seat decides to pass, opener, with a minimum opening (13-16 VPs) will pass and the contract will be in 3-spades, a part-score requiring 9 tricks. *Lessons Learned: As responder, holding 4-card support you would be very interested in knowing if the opening bid was a little more than a minimum. For example, if opener holds 17 VPs, his combined hand would have 25 VPs, enough for a game in Spades. The bid for learning the opener's strength is the cuebid which signals support, interest in reaching game and 10 or more. With only 8 VPs, the cue bid is not available. A discussion as to what opener should do if the Fourth Seat's advance is at the 3-level in Notrump or the 4-level in a suit is beyond beginning bridge. What is not beyond beginning bridge is awareness that, if opener has Minimum opening strength (13-16) and responder has a weak hand, it is likely that the opponents' strength is relatively equal to the combined strength of the opening side. In that scenario, if the other side goes to 3-notrump, signaling 9 trumps in their combined hand and the opening side has 9 trumps; the Law of Total Tricks would hold that neither side can make 10 tricks.*

CHAPTER 7
QUIZ # 4 CONTINUED
THIRD SEAT RESPONDS TO A VARIETY OF OPENING BIDS

SCENARIO # 3: OPENING IN 1-CLUB, PASS IN SECOND SEAT, RESPONSE AS THIRD SEAT?

K x x x
x x
x x
A Q x x x

Commentary # 5: You respond in 1-spade. This unbalanced shape has 10VPs, derived from 9 HCPs+1LP for the 5-card Clubs. Responder's first priority, even with support for the minor suit opening, is to introduce a major suit as a "New Suit," a forcing bid. The 5-card Club suit in Responder identifies with some certainty that there is at least an 8-card Club fit in the combined hand. The 1-spade New Suit response signals 6+VPs and at least a 4-card Spade suit. Since opener did not open in Spades, he clearly does not have a 5-card Spade suit. However, the possibility of a 4—4 match in Spades is a possibility. The combined hand has at least 23 VPs (at least 13 in the opening and 10 VPs known in the responder). Since the Second Seat passed, it is likely the Auction is non-competitive. *Lessons Learned: Opener's rebid will determine if play in a major suit is likely. With 4-card support for Responder's Spades as a proposed new trump suit, opener can raise to show a fit in the combined hand. Since the combined hand has at least 23VPs, there may be enough to go for a bonus level, including a part-score or game bid. However, opener's rebid is necessary to determine if there is an 8-card fit in Spades and where the opener is in his 13-21VP range. The guidance, with a 4-card Spade suit is for the opener's rebid at the cheapest level, 2-spades, signals the 4—4 match as well as a point-count of 13-15VPs. A rebid of 3-spades would signal 16-18VPs and a 4-spade rebid signals 19+VPs. If we assume that the opener's rebid is 3-spades, the responder does the math and calculates a combined hand of at least 26VPs (16 in the opener and 10 in the responder), enough for game in a major. Responder's final bid will be 4-spades, game, which is where he wanted to be from the beginning of the Auction.*

x x x
Q J x
K x x
K Q x x

Commentary # 6: You respond in 2-notrump. Your partner's opening bid signals 13-21 VPs and at least a 3-card Club suit. Your perfectly balanced 4-3-3-3 shape has 11 HCPs, an intermediate strength hand with Stoppers in at least 3 of the suits. As Responder, you estimate the combined hand to have at least 24 VPs, enough for a bonus level in a part-score or game. With the opening in a minor and no 4-card major suit to introduce as a trump suit, your next priority is to respond in Notrump ahead of a trump suit in a minor. With responder holding 11 VPs, the guidance is to respond to a 1-level opening in a minor suit in 2-notrump, an invitational jump bid since it is one level higher than necessary. *Lessons Learned: Opener's acceptance of the 2-Notrump invitation to game is based on holding more than 13VPs since 25VPs are necessary for game in Notrump.*

CHAPTER 7
QUIZ # 4 CONTINUED
THIRD SEAT RESPONDS TO A VARIETY OF OPENING BIDS

SCENARIO # 4: OPENING IN 2-HEARTS, SECOND SEAT PASSES, RESPONSE AS THIRD SEAT?

A K Q J x
Q J x
Q x x
x x

Commentary # 7: You double jump to 4-hearts, in response to a weak-two opening in Hearts: When responding to preemptive openings, the guidance is to rely on the total trump counts in the combined hand, not point-counts. With Hearts as trump, the Law of Total Tricks suggests it is safe to bid to the 3-level, requiring 9 tricks. However, the very strong side suit in Spades should provide the extra needed trick to make a game bid. Also, responder deduces that the combined hand is strong in Hearts since the opening bid signals a good suit that must include some combination of the Heart AK10 necessary to make the 6-card suit good. *Lessons learned: This is an excellent example of responder, with a strong hand, taking advantage of the precise description provided by the Weak-Two bid and taking the offensive with an aggressive, but justified jump to game. While the Law of Total Tricks applies only to the number of trump cards in the combined hand, responder correctly identified his very strong side suit in Spades (a non-trump suit) and determined that a game bid in Hearts is appropriate.*

x
x x
Q x x x x
Q x x x x

Commentary # 8: You will pass. This very unbalanced 5-5-2-1 shape has 6 VPs, two 5-card minor suits and no support for the Weak-Two opening in Hearts. Since the Weak-Two can be opened with a range of 5-10VPs, the combined hand has 16VPs *at the most*. This indicates that the other side has the majority of the strength, probably all concentrated in the fourth seat since the second seat passed. Since the Weak-Two opening already commits the side to making 8 tricks, the responder should avoid taking the bidding higher. Despite the identified 8-card fit in Hearts, responder does not hold a single sure winner. *Lessons Learned: While the Law of Total Tricks indicates that the side may safely bid to the 2-level, requiring 8 tricks, responder's hand provides no basis for raising the opening bid. Actually, making 8 tricks will be a challenge if the other side passes.*

CHAPTER 7
QUIZ #4 CONTINUED
THIRD SEAT RESPONDS TO A VARIETY OF OPENING BIDS

SCENARIO #5: OPENING IN 1-SPADE, SECOND SEAT PASSES, RESPONSE AS THIRD SEAT?

x x
x x x
A K
K x x x x x

Commentary # 9: You respond to the 1-spade opening in 2-Clubs: Responder, with a 2-card Spade suit is unable to meet his first priority, which is to support the opening in 1-spade. The second priority would be to introduce Hearts, the other major, as a New Suit, but that would require a 5-card Heart suit, which is not available. With an unbalanced hand, not suitable for Notrump and both majors unavailable, the next possible trump suit would be the 6-card Club suit at the 2-level. *Lessons Learned: With play in Notrump and a major suit ruled out, it would appear that the best contract in a minor suit is a better alternative than a pass from the Responder. Responding in a New Suit at the 2-level requires 11 or more and a 4-card or longer suit.*

SCENARIO # 6: OPENING IN 2-CLUBS, SECOND SEAT PASSES; RESPONSE AS THIRD SEAT?

K Q 10 x x
K x x
Q x x
x x

Commentary # 10: You will make an "immediate positive response" in 2-Spades: Since the opening is an artificial, strong 2-club bid signaling 22+VPs, the guidance is for the responder, with 8+VPs to make an immediate response if he holds a good 5-card or longer suit, or, to respond in 2-notrump to show a balanced hand. Since the response is in 2-spades; and, since Responder holds 11VPs derived from 10HCPs+1LP for the 5-card Spade suit, the estimated strength in the combined hand is at least 33VPs, more than enough for game. The only question is the "where" part and that depends on whether the opener has support for Responder's 2-spade response, signaling his longest and highest ranking suit. *Lessons Learned: If opener has at least 3-card support, an 8-card fit is identified and the side, with at least 33VPs in the combined hand should go to game. If opener does not like Spades, but has a 5-card Heart suit he can rebid it at the 3-level; or, with a suitable hand, opener could rebid in 3-notrump, game. Without Slam Bidding skills, beginners should cap their bids at the 4-level with a major suit game bid and at the 3-level with a Notrump game bid. With this strength in the combined hand, it is likely you will make more than what is required for game. In Rubber Scoring, you will earn the TSPs for all the tricks you make based on the strain played as long as they are more than what was bid.*

CHAPTER 7
QUIZ # 4-CONTINUED
THE THIRD SEAT REACTS TO A VARIETY OF OPENING BIDS

SCENARIO #7: OPENING IN 1-NOTRUMP, SECOND SEAT PASSES; RESPONSE AS THIRD SEAT?

K Q x x x
x x x
x x x
x x

Commentary # 11: You respond in 2-hearts, a transfer bid signaling at least a 5-card Spade suit: The Transfer Convention permits a Transfer even if the Responder has Zero points. In this case, Responder only has 6 VPs derived from 5 HCPs+1 LP for the 5-card suit. Because of the Transfer Convention, opener is required to take the transfer, usually by rebidding in 2-spades, regardless of the number of Spades he may hold. However, if the opener is at the top of his opening ranges (17HCPs) with a 4-card Spade suit, he can take the Transfer by rebidding in 3-spades, a highly Invitational bid. The requirement for the opener to "take the Transfer" is necessary to keep the stronger hand hidden. The Responder now has his opportunity to describe his hand's strength. Since the opener took the Transfer at the 3-level, signaling 17HCPs and a 4-card Spade suit, Responder now estimates the combined hand to have 23VPs, not enough for game and passes. Since responder's pass is followed by a 3rd consecutive pass, the final bid is 3-spades, a part-score contract, requiring 9 tricks. The bidding sequence is as follows:

Round # 1:   1-notrump---pass---2-hearts---pass

Round # 2:   3-spades---pass---pass---pass

Lessons Learned: Responder, holding only 6 VPs should be happy to pass 3-spades because the combined hand is limited to only 23 VPs and a 9-trick contract is a more likely to make than a game contract.

SCENARIO # 8: OPENING IN 1-DIAMOND, SECOND SEAT PASSES, RESPONSE AS THIRD SEAT?

K x x
A K Q J x
Q x x
K x

Commentary # 12: You respond in 2-hearts: This balanced shape, with 19HCPs (18 HCPs+1LP) is strong enough for a **JUMP SHIFT** response to a minor suit opening at the 1-level. The guidance for the Jump Shift response is 17+VPs and a good 5-card or more Heart or Spade suit. The combined hand has at least 32VPs, much more than enough for game. *Lessons Learned: It is always the priority of the Responder to an opening in a minor to respond in a major suit. With a Jump Shift in your bidding agreement, a 2-heart response to a 1-level minor suit opening signals at least 30VPs and at least a 5-card major suit to the opener. In beginning bridge, which does not include Slam Bidding skills, the bidding is capped at the 4-level for a game bid in a major. If opener holds a 4-card Heart suit, he identifies at least a 9-card fit which the Law of Total Tricks would support to the 3-level. Only the opener knows where his strength is within the opening suit range of 13-21VPs; and, whether to go to 4-hearts, game or keep the bidding at the 3-level.*

CHAPTER 7
QUIZ # 4 CONTINUED
THIRD SEAT REACTS TO A VARIETY OF OPENING BIDS

SCENARIO # 9: OPENING IN 1-SPADE, SECOND SEAT PASSES, RESPONSE AS THE THIRD SEAT?

K x x
K Q x x x
Q x x
x x

Commentary # 13: You respond in 2-hearts: This balanced shape has 11 VPs (10 HCPs+1LP). Responder estimates the combined hand to have at least 24VPs (13 in the opener and 11 known in the responder); part-score or game bonus is in sight. With only 3-card support for Spades, the guidance, with 11-12VPs, is to bid a new 4-card or longer suit at the cheapest level. At the next opportunity to bid, responder supports the opening in Spades by rebidding 3-spades, signaling an intermediate hand. Now, opener knows that the support is only 3-cards; and, that the responder has at least 11VPs. If partner has more than minimum opening strength he will go to game in 4-spades. Of course, with only 8 Spade trumps identified in the combined hand, the side will need to develop extra tricks. To do that, a strong side suit will be helpful. *Lesson Learned: The guidance to bid a New Suit permits responder to signal his intermediate hand and limit his support to the 3-card level. This provides opener with all the information he needs as to whether or not he should support the New Suit and if there is enough of a point-count to go to game.*

CHAPTER 8

FOURTH SEAT ADVANCES OVERCALLS AND TAKEOUT DOUBLES

AT LAST! THE FOURTH SEAT GETS HIS "15 SECONDS OF FAME"

The Fourth Seat, AKA the **ADVANCER,** makes the last call in the first round of a bidding sequence. The Fourth and the Third Seats share a similar role: to respond to their partners' suit bids with at least 3-card support; and, without 3-card support, to introduce a New Suit. As a result, much of the guidance provided the Advancer in this Chapter will be somewhat similar to that provided Responder in Chapter 7.

ADVANCING OVERCALLS IN A MAJOR WITH 3+CARD SUPPORT AND WEAK HAND

When advancing partner's Overcall, the first three seats have had the opportunity to make an opening bid, an Overcall or a Double and a response to an opening bid. In the following Scenario, the Fourth Seat is advancing a 1-level Overcall. When it is the Fourth Seat's turn to Advance, he must be aware of "how high" the level of bidding has become since that affects the cheapest level available for a legal advance:

SCENARIO: With 6-9VPs, a weak hand, the Fourth Seat, with 3-card or more Support for a 1-level Overcall which always signals a good 5-card or longer suit, makes an Advance at a level based on the following guidance developed from the Law of Total Tricks:

- With 3-card support, at least an 8-card fit is identified, permitting a Raise to the 2-level. Since the Overcall is at the 1-level, this is a non-Jump, non-Preemptive Raise since it is not made 1 level higher than what is necessary to be legal.

- With 4-card support, at least a 9-card fit is identified, permitting a double Jump Raise to the 3-level. Since the Overcall is at the 1-level, this is a Preemptive Raise because it is made 2 levels higher than necessary.

- With 5-card support, at least a 10-card fit is identified, permitting a triple Jump raise to the 4-level. Because the Overcall is at the 1-level, this is a Preemptive Raise since it is made 3 levels higher than necessary.

While all three of the above advances are made with the same level of strength, 6-9VPs, the degree of Support for the Overcall suit (3-card, 4-card or 5-card suits) determines the level of the Raises and are based on the Law of Total Tricks which indicates it is safe to Raise to the level of the combined trumps held by the side. Since Advances are not forcing, partner may or may not reply. The solution to that dilemma is the **CUEBID** and is discussed further in this Chapter.

CAUTION: UNDERTANDING THE LIMITATIONS OF THE LAW OF TOTAL TRICKS

The above guidance on bidding levels is not based on point-counts; rather, it is based on the Law of Total Tricks, a theory popularized by Larry Cohen. This theory suggests that it is usually safe to Raise the level of bidding to the number of trumps held in the side's combined hand. The theory should not be interpreted to mean that a specified number of tricks will be safely made when the bidding is maintained at the Law's suggested level. While advancer may or may not make the number of tricks suggested by the Law of Total Tricks, it may be better to make the bid and go down than letting the opponents take the bid. Further, following the bidding levels suggested by this theory may push the other side to bid higher than they normally would have bid.

ADVANCING THE SUIT OVERCALL WITH A CUEBID

THE PROBLEM

In the above Scenario not much discussion is needed to arrive at the level of the Advance. The Law of Total Tricks supports bidding levels based on the number of trump cards in the combined hand. As a result, there is not much bidding conversation required to determine the Overcaller's strength. Of course not all scenarios are as accommodating as the one described above.

While the overcall always requires at least a good 5-card suit, it can be bid at both the 1-level with 7-12 HCPs; and, at the 2-level with 13-17 VPs. The problem, when overcaller holds 13-17 VPs, is that he more than likely will overcall at the 1-level in order to provide Bidding Space for his partner's participation in the Auction. When overcalls are made with 13-17 VPs they are said to be a **MAXIMUM** and with 7-12 HCPs, a **MINIMUM.** So, how does an Advancer know when his partner's 1-level Overcall is made with Maximum or Minimum strength?

Here's what the bidding could look like before the Advancer Cuebids in the opponents' suit with 10+VPs:

Round #1: 1-heart---1-spade---pass---?

SCENARIO: You are in the Fourth Seat, holding 12 VPs and at least 3-card support for the 1-spade overcall. Since you have identified at least an 8-card Spade fit in the combined hand, you are now very interested in knowing if your partner's overcall was made while holding Maximum Strength, defined as 13-17VPs. If overcaller has 13 VPs, with your 12 VPs, there is enough in the combined hand to make a Game Bid. Since Advances are not forcing, the Fourth Seat needs a bid that requires the Overcaller to describe his hand's strength.

THE SOLUTION

The solution to the dilemma discussed above is the Cuebid, a bid made by Advancer in the opponents' suit when actually holding 10+ VPs and at least 3-card Support for the Overcall. Since, according to the above scenario, the Fourth Seat actually holds 12 VPs, he has a very solid Cuebid.

THE CUEBID BIDDING CONVERSATION

This is what the bidding like when advancer Cuebids the Overcall:

Round #1: 1-heart---1-spade---pass---2-hearts

Round #2 pass---4-spades---pass---pass

Round #3: pass

The Cuebid Bidding Conversation in Round #1starts with the 2-heart Cuebid, a bid in the opponents' suit and says the following:

Advancer to Overcaller: "I have 10+ VPs and 3-card or more support; and, that gives us at least an 8-card Spade fit in the combined hand. What I need to know is if your Overcall was made in with 13-17 VPs. If so, I am telling you we have enough strength for a Game Bid in Spades. Since my Cuebid is forcing, I am expecting you to give me a reply that is descriptive enough to tell me if we can go to game."

Overcaller: "I can do better than that because I actually hold 15 VPs and a good 5-card Spade suit. Your Cuebid tells me that you have 10 or more and 3-card Support. This is my rebid and it is as descriptive as I can make it: 4-spades, game. My best estimate of our combined hand is that we have at least an 8-card fit in Spades, and that means we need to develop 2 extra tricks. Wish me luck since it looks like I am the Declarer."

ADVANCING THE OVERCALL WITHOUT A CUEBID

When the overcall is in 1-spade and advancer only holds 8 VPs, the Cuebid cannot be employed since it requires 10+VPs. However, if advancer holds 4-card support and even with zero points he can make a Preemptive Jump to 3-spades, requiring 9 tricks. In that scenario, if the overcaller has 15 points and the advancer has zero points, it is clear that the other side has enough for game. While your side does not have the strength to make 9 tricks, the Law of Total Tricks permits the jump to 3-spades so that your side can prevent the other side from getting to game. As previously discussed, making the bid based on the LAW and failing may be better than letting the other side take the bid.

ADVANCING THE 1-NOTRUMP OVERCALL WITH A TRANSFER BID OR A STAYMAN

Following a 1-level Opening in a major, Second Seat Overcalls in 1-notrump with 15-18 HCPs; and, a Suitable Hand with *length and strength in the opening suit bid* along with stoppers in two other suits. Since the Opening signals a 5-card major, *the Opening Lead card is likely to be in the Opening suit bid.* As a result, the Notrump overcall needs added protection to prevent against a run. The guidance provides for that protection by requiring that the "length and strength in the opening suit bid" includes at least a 3-card suit preferably headed by two stoppers in the opening suit bid.

SCENARIO: The opening is in 1-heart, and the 1-notrump Overcall is made with 17 HCPs and a Suitable Hand including "length and strength in the opening suit bid." As you will see, the guidance for the Advancer when partner Overcalls in notrump is the same as the guidance given the Responder when the Opening is in Notrump.

Round # 1: 1-heart---1-notrump---pass---2-clubs.

An Advance in 2-clubs, following a Notrump Overcall is a Stayman. Overcaller knows that his combined hand holds at least enough for game in a major (17 HCPs in his hand and at least 8 HCPs with the Stayman). The balance of the bidding conversation is primarily between the Overcaller and the Advancer as they try to identify a 4—4 major suit fit. The protocol for doing that is presented in Chapter 7 this is what the next rounds of bidding look like:

Round # 2: pass---2-spades---pass--- 3-spades

Overcaller rebids 2-spades identifying Spades as the only 4-card major he holds; Advancer's rebid, at the 3-level to be legal, signals that he also has a 4-card Spade suit. Since Advancer estimates the combined hand to have 23 VPs, not enough for game, his rebid is in 3-spades, an Invitational Bid.

Round # 3: pass---4-spades---pass---pass

When it is the overcaller's turn to estimate the strength in his combined hand, Overcaller, holding 17HCPs, estimated the Fourth Seat to have at least 8HCPs in order to bid the 2-club Stayman and the side to have 25 VPs. With that, the Second Seat goes to game in 4-spades without any further conversation.

Round # 4: pass

The 4th round is shown to display the third and final pass needed to make the final bid a 4-spade Contract requiring 10 tricks.

ADVANCING THE 1-NOTRUMP OVERCALL IN 2-NOTRUMP

When the Overcall is in 1-notrump, following a suit opening and neither a Stayman nor a Transfer is available, the next priority is to Advance the 1-notrump Overcall in 2-notrump. A Balanced Hand is not required to respond to a Notrump Overcall in Notrump.

The guidance for advancing a Notrump Overcall in Notrump *is the same as responding to a Notrump Opening Bid in Notrump*: the Advancer needs 8-9VPs to respond in 2-notrump; and, with 10+VPs to respond in 3-notrump. The Bidding Sequence looks like this when Advancer holds 10VPs:

Round #1:   1-diamond---1-notrump---pass---2-notrump

Round #2:   pass---3-notrump---pass---pass

Round #3:   pass

Opener's 3-notrump rebid in Round # 2 is a game contract signaling that he is satisfied that the combined hand has at least 25VPs, enough for game in Notrump.

ADVANCING THE DOUBLE WITH A SUIT

The difference between an Opening suit bid and a Takeout Double is that the Opening bid names a suit and a bidding level, while the Double names neither and asks partner to select a trump suit from his longest *unbid* suit. The Double promises 3-card or more support for any unbid suit except when the Double is made with the 4-4-3-2 Shape and the partner selects the 2-card suit as the trump suit. Since the doubler is the only one who knows if advancer's selection of a trump suit will result in a 7-card imperfect fit, the doubler may rebid in Notrump to avoid it and the game will be played in Notrump. *Finally, when the Double immediately follows an Opening in a major, the Doubler almost always promises 4-cards in the other major.*

While Opening Bids and Overcalls are capped at the top of their ranges, the Double has no upper point-count limit. Since the double goes nowhere until Advancer selects an unbid trump suit, the Advancer is forced to select a trump suit, even when he has no points. Before the Fourth Seat can advance his partner's Double, he must determine the "how high and where" parts of his bid. The guidance for doing that is as follows:

- Where? Select the longest suit among the unbid suits; prefer a major over a minor suit With suits of equal length always choose the senior suit

- How high? With 0-8VPs bid the unbid suit at the cheapest level available; with 9-11VPs jump one level, invitational; and with 12+VPs get the side to game since the combined hand has at least 25 VPs.

ADVANCING THE DOUBLE IN NOTRUMP

Why in the world would Advancer, who has been asked by the Doubler to select an unbid trump suit, choose to advance in Notrump? The simple answer: when Advancer's longest unbid suit is in a minor. The priority, when play in a major is not available, is to play in Notrump, always ahead of playing in a minor. Here is a good example of a hand that qualifies for advancing the Double in Notrump when the Opening is in 1-diamond and the first Round looks like this:

Round # 1:   1-diamond----double----pass---2-notrump

K 8 3
8 7 6
K J 3 2
A 9 8

Note that advancer's balanced 4-3-3-3 shape has *length and strength in the opening suit bid which also includes 2 stoppers,* as well as stoppers in two of the other three suits. The level of the Advance in 2-Notrump is based on the following strength levels:

- 6-10 VPs, advance in 1-notrump at the cheapest level

- 11-12 VPs, jump advance in 2-notrump, an Invitational Bid. The combined hand has at least 24 VPs and doubler can determine if he wants to go to part-score or game in Notrump

- 13+VPs, advancer should go to game in 3-notrump since the combined hand has at least 26 VPs.

As previously discussed, there is no need to bid beyond the 3-notrump level since the Total Point Score yield is based on tricks made.

ADVANCING THE DOUBLE IN A CUEBID

Since a Double usually requires at least 13 VPs, the Advancer, holding 13 VPs and a 4-card Spade suit knows there is enough strength in the combined hand for game in a major. Of course, Advancer cannot go straight to game in Spades since that might land him into a 7-card Imperfect Fit. Rather, the Advancer's priority is to determine if there is an 8-card or longer major suit Spade fit in the combined hand. Since the Opening bid was in 1-club, the Advancer can Cuebid in 2-clubs, the cheapest level, signaling 10 or more points, interest in a Part-score or game and demanding a descriptive reply from the Doubler. The first Round looks like this:
:
Round # 1:   1-club---double---pass---2-clubs

In this Scenario, it is the Doubler who first proposes a trump suit. With a 4-card Spade suit as his best and longest major suit, the Doubler rebids in 2-spades. Advancer, holding 13 VPs, now identifies an 8-card Spade fit and Jumps to game in 4-spades. The bidding goes like this:

Round # 2:   pass---2-spades---pass---4-spades

If doubler's rebid had not resulted in an 8-card Spade fit, Advancer may go to game in 3-notrump with a Suitable Hand.

WHEN THE ADVANCER PASSES A TAKEOUT DOUBLE

A Double, immediately following an Opening suit bid is a ticking time bomb. While it is clearly understood to be for Takeout, it is legally a Double for Penalty until it is "taken out." So, if the First Seat opens, for example, in 1-heart and the Second Seat Doubles, followed by passes from the Third and Fourth Seats, Opener can make the third consecutive pass, allowing him to play in a cheaply acquired 1-heart contract **DOUBLED FOR PENALTY.**

That contract could be a serious problem for the Advancer's relationship with the Doubler since the contract is likely made and the other side will earn double the points they would have earned in an undoubled contract: an unfavorable outcome which the Fourth Seat created by passing when he should have bid. The bidding could look like this:

Round # 1:   1-heart---double---pass---pass

Round # 2:   pass

The final contract is in 1-heart, doubled for penalty.

However, if the Third Seat supports the Opening, he has taken out the Double for Penalty, thereby allowing the Fourth Seat to pass if he chooses to do so without creating a contract, inadvertently Doubled for Penalty.

SCENARIO: A Bidding Sequence starts with an Opening in a major; followed by a Double and a Raise by the third Seat to the 2-level, signaling at least 3-card support and 6-10VPs: the bidding looks like this:

Round # 1:   1-heart---double---2-hearts---?

What would you do as the advancer with the following hand?

```
x x
J x x
x x x
Jx x x x
```

This hand has 3 unbid suits (Spades, Diamonds and Clubs); it is also a 3VP hand that is going nowhere. So, is there any way the advancer can pass without bringing a Penalty Double on the partnership? The simple answer is yes, because the advancer's RHO has made a bid (the Raise to 2-hearts) which "takes out" the Double for Penalty.

However, if the Advancer's RHO (the Third Seat) had not bid, the time bomb would still be ticking and the bidding would look like this:

Round # 1:   1-heart---double---pass---?

Now, the Advancer has two choices: make a bid to take out the Double; or, pass and likely have the openers play in 1-hearts, doubled for penalty. Since a Double is forcing, the advancer, even with zero points must respond. With only 3VPs, the advancer is in a poor position to compete, but compete he must. An advance at the cheapest level possible, 2-clubs, would take out the Double for Penalty, but would require 8 tricks if played. The combined hand could have as little as 16VPs (13 in Doubler and 13 known in Advancer). The Doubler's rebid will decide how poorly the side will fare.

WHEN THE FOURTH SEAT BALANCES

When the First Seat makes an opening bid and the next two seats pass, any bid made by the Fourth Seat is a **BALANCING BID,** also known as a **REOPENING BID** since the opponents' bidding has stopped at a low level. The bidding could look like this:

Round # 1:   1-heart---pass---pass---?

If the Fourth Seat passes, the Auction is over. However, since partner in the Second Seat may have passed with good values but no bid that conforms to his bidding agreement, the Fourth Seat may find it advisable to bid, even when **LIGHT,** an elegant way of describing a hand with less than Opening Strength.

As indicated, the alternative to not making a Balancing Bid is to pass and abandon a combined hand that may have enough strength to compete. When the Fourth Seat makes a light bid in this scenario that Reopening Bid can be in a suit, in Notrump, or a Double for Takeout. For example, the guidance for making a 1-notrump Balancing Bid is a Suitable Hand and 11-14HCPs and the bidding could look like this:

Round # 1:   1-heart---pass---pass---1-notrump

When the Balancer's partner, the Second Seat has an opportunity to bid, his guidance would be the same as responding to a 1-notrump Opening Bid; that is, he could use the Stayman or a Transfer, recognizing that the bid is in a maximum of 14HCPs.

Beginner is cautioned that Balancing usually requires advanced skills, because other bids, when made in the "passout seat" have different meanings. As a minimum, this Scenario should be discussed in the "Bidding Agreement Conversation" because it is likely that the beginner will encounter such a situation while occupying the Fourth Seat with less than Opening Strength.

ENDING BEGINNING BRIDGE'S TOUR OF THE FOUR SEATS

With this Chapter, we conclude the review of the four different seat assignments Beginner assumes in Contract Social Bridge. As may be apparent, required bridge skills become more interesting when responding as the Third Seat or advancing as the Fourth Seat. While the perception is that Advancing may be complex, there is a great deal of similarity in the guidance to the 2 Seats. Clearly, Beginning Bridge is a cumulative journey with each step building on the previous one. You are to be congratulated on making it this far. You are not the same person you were at the beginning of this journey. The end of the Beginning is in sight.

CHAPTER 8
QUIZ # 5
ADVANCING OVERCALLS AND TAKEOUT DOUBLES

SCENARIO: While the Bidding and 2-hand Card Diagrams presented below will vary with each quiz problem, the following are constants: South and North are Opener and Responder, respectively; West and East are Overcaller/Doubler and Advancer, respectively. The challenge, in all problems is the same: What is East's advance to West's Overcall or Double while considering the level of North's bid in order to be legal.

In Real Bridge East, of course does not have visibility of West's hand. Again, the main challenge in this quiz is East's call. At this point, the only information East has relating to the other three hidden hands is from the Bidding Conversation:

WEST	NORTH	EAST	SOUTH
			1-C
1-H	2-C	?	

WEST	EAST
x x x	x x x
K Q J x x	A x x
Q x x	x x x x x
x x	Q x

Commentary # 1: East advances West's 1-heart Overcall in 2-hearts: West's Simple Suit Overcall, signals 7-17HCPs and a good 5-card Heart suit or a 6-card or more Heart suit. North's Raise of the opening suit bid to the 2-level signals at least 3-card support and a weak 6-10VP hand. East, with 3-card Support identifies at least an 8-card fit in Hearts. The challenge for East is not only to advance partner's Overcall but to do it in a bid that outranks North's 2-club Raise. With 6-9VPs and 3-card support, the guidance is for East to advance partner's overcall in 2-hearts, a bid that, if final, would require 8 tricks. The advance is recognized by the Overcaller as a Non-Preemptive bid made with a weak hand at the cheapest level available. If East's Advance is the final bid, West becomes the Declarer and East the dummy. *Lessons Learned: East's bid of 2-hearts is based on the Law of Total Trucks, which states that the side should bid to the level of the number of trumps in the combined hand, which in this scenario are 8 trumps. The Law does not suggest that 8 tricks will be safely made because 8 trump cards are identified in the combined hand; only that it should be safe to bid to the 2-level with 8 trumps in the combined hand. In the end, only the Play of the Tricks will determine if the 8 tricks will be made.*

CHAPTER 8
QUIZ # 5 CONTINUED
ADVANCING OVERCALLS AND TAKEOUT DOUBLES

SEE ABOVE SCENARIO

WEST	NORTH	EAST	SOUTH
			1-D
1-H	PASS	?	

```
          WEST              EAST
          x x x             A Q J x x
          A Q 10 x x        J x
          A                 K x x
          K Q J x           x x x
```

Commentary # 2: East advances in 2-spades: West's Overcall of the opening bid in a minor suit signals a good 5-card or more Heart suit and 7-17HCPs. Since East does not have at least 3-card support for partner's Hearts, his guidance is to introduce the other major, Spades as a New Suit. The guidance for advancing in a New Suit requires at least a good 5-card Spade suit or a 6-card or longer Spade suit and 11+VPs for a 2-level advance. With that guidance met, East's advance is 2-spades.

For training purpose, let's assume that NS will no longer compete in the auction and, it is now West's opportunity to show his 3-card Support for partner's Spades. In doing so, West identifies at least an 8-card fit in Spades and becomes the likely dummy. West calculates his hand's strength to be 17 VPs and estimates the combined hand to have at least 28VPs; and, with at least an 8-card fit identified goes to 4-spades, game.

After 3 consecutive passes, the final contract is 4-spades and the Declarer is identified as East since he was the first player to mention Spades. When the final pass is made, that is the cue for the opening lead to be made and for West to makes his dummy hand visible. East, for the first time, sees his combined hand which has 29 VPs (17 in West and 12 in East). East also Tallies his side's Sure Winners to determine if he has enough tricks to fulfill his contract: 1 in Spades, 1 in Hearts, 2 in Diamonds; and, 2 Delayed Winners in Clubs. Since the total Sure Winners are 4, the Declarer, West, needs to promote his 2 Delayed Winners develop 2 extra tricks in order to simply fulfill his contract. *Lessons Learned: At this point, it is time to formulate a plan that will develop as many tricks as possible. The bridge skill for developing tricks is based on the Declarer's Analysis of his combined hand and his Plan of the Play, defined as the mental process by which Declarer decides how to use assets of the combined hand to fulfill the contract, develop overtricks and minimize penalties. In the end, whether winners are "sure winners", "delayed winners" or "developed winners", the only winners that count are those that take tricks in the Play of the Tricks.*

CHAPTER 8
QUIZ # 5 CONTINUED
ADVANCING OVERCALLS AND TAKEOUT DOUBLES

WEST	NORTH	EAST	SOUTH
			1-D
1-S	Pass	?	

WEST	EAST
A K J x x x x	x x x
x x	A K x
x x	x x x
A Q	K J x x

Commentary # 3: East Cuebids in 2-diamonds: East's priority as the advancer is to support partner's Simple Suit Overcall at the 1-level, signaling 7-17VPs. East, with 11 HCPs and 3-card support in Spades, is interested in Part-Score or game if partner has Opening Strength or better. In order to determine the actual strength in West's overcall, East uses the forcing Cuebid which requires at least 3-card support and strength (at least 10VPs). The guidance is to always make the Cuebid at the cheapest level available, 2-diamonds in this Scenario. Overcaller's responsibility is to provide Cuebidder with a rebid that is descriptive enough to indicate whether his overcall was made with Minimum or Maximum strength.

Since the Cuebid signals at least 3-card Support, Overcaller, with a good 7-card Spades, estimates the combined hand to have at least 10 trumps in the combined hand. The OEB indicates that a simple way to use the Law of Total Tricks is to always bid to the level of your side's number of trumps. Based on that guidance, West rebids in 4-spades, a game bid requiring 10 tricks. Since West first mentioned Spades, he becomes the Declarer and East the Dummy.

Once the combined hand becomes visible, the Declarer counts the Sure Winner in EW is as follows: Spades, 2; Hearts 2, Diamonds, Zero; and, Clubs 4 for a total of 8 sure winners. Based on that Tally, 2 extra tricks are needed to fulfill the contract. With a 7-card Spade suit in the Declarer it would appear that the 2 extra needed tricks can be developed though promotion. *Lessons Learned: East's Cuebid effectively tells his partner everything he needs to know about his partner's 10+VP hand, Support for Spades and interest in part-score or game. More importantly, the Cuebid requires the advancer to not only reply, but to reply descriptively. Even if West's overcall was made with minimum strength, a 10 card Spade fit would have still been identified (7-card suit known in his hand and at least a 3-card suit in the cuebidder) and the Law of Total Tricks would have supported a 4-spade game bid, requiring 10 tricks. Once again, the Law of Total Tricks does not state that 10 tricks will be safely made if there are 10 trumps in the combined hand. Only the play of the tricks will determine whether the game contract will be made.*

CHAPTER 8
QUIZ # 5 CONTINUED
ADVANCING OVERCALLS AND TAKEOUT DOUBLES

WEST	NORTH	EAST	SOUTH
			1-D
DBL	PASS	?	

WEST	EAST
A K 10 x	Q J x
x x x x	A Q x x
x	A x x
A K x x	x x x

Commentary # 4: East advances the Double with a Cuebid in 2-diamonds: West, following an opening bid in 1-diamond, immediately challenges with a Double, signaling opening strength at least 3-card support, preferably 4-card support, in any one of the unbid suits. West's Double also asks partner to select the side's trump suit from the 3 unbid suits (Spades, Hearts and Clubs).

East estimates the combined hand to have at least 26VPs, (at least 13 in the Doubler and 13 known in his hand) enough for game in a major. While East is expected to select a trump suit from the 3 unbid suits, his immediate challenge is to help the Doubler estimate the game strength in the combined EW hand. East does just that by advancing in 2-diamonds, a forcing Cuebid showing interest in game.

Now that West knows of East's interest in a game contract, he will likely start by rebidding in 2-spades, the longest and senior ranking suit in his hand. With only 3-card support for partner's Spades, East looks for an alternative to playing in a 7-card imperfect fit in Spades. With 4-cards in Hearts and opening strength, East rebids in 3-hearts, a forcing bid. West, with 4-card support for Hearts identifies at least an 8-card fit in Hearts and, as the likely dummy, revalues his hand for shortness, adding 3DPs for the singleton in Diamonds. West now estimates the combined hand to have at least 27VPs (17 known in his hand and at least 10 with the Cuebidder) and descriptively goes to game in 4-hearts. *Lessons Learned: While the Cuebid is usually bid by Advancer to determine the strength of his partner's overcall, in this case Advancer already knew that his partner held at least opening strength. As a result, EW were able to keep the bidding low as they go about avoiding a 7-card imperfect fit in Spades and finding the "Golden" 8-card fit in Hearts. Once West makes his 4-heart game rebid, East will pass since bidding is capped for beginners without bidding skills.*

Once the dummy becomes visible, East, the Declarer, tallies his Sure Winners: Spades, 4; Hearts, 1; Diamonds, 1; and, Clubs, 2; for a total of 8 sure winners, indicating a need for 2 extra tricks. Since the final contract promises 10 tricks, the defense only needs 4 tricks to set the EW contract. In the end, the play of the tricks determines whether EW fulfills the contract or NS sets it.

CHAPTER 8
QUIZ #5
ADVANCING OVERCALLS AND TAKEOUT DOUBLES

BIDDING DIAGRAM # 5

WEST	NORTH	EAST	SOUTH
			1-D
DBL	PASS	?	

WEST	EAST
A K 10 x	x x
x x x x	K x x
x	A K x x x
A K 10 x	Q J x

Commentary # 5: East advances in 3-notrump: West, immediately following the Opening in 1-diamond, challenges with a Double. East estimates the combined hand to have at least 27 VPs, (14 known in East and at least 13 in West) enough for game in a major or in Notrump. At this point, there is no question that there will be a game bid; rather, the question is "where?" With no 4-card or longer major available, East's next priority is to play in Notrump ahead of a minor suit. The guidance for a Notrump advance requires a balanced hand with Length and strength in the opening suit bid; and, stoppers in two other suits. Additionally, the guidance suggests that the level of the advance is based on the strength in the Advancer: with 6-10VPs for a 1-level advance in Notrump, 11-12VPs for a 2-level advance in Notrump; and, with 13+VPs the advance is in 3-notrump. Since East's hand meets the guidance, he advances in 3-notrump game, requiring 9 tricks. *Lessons Learned: Advancing a Double in Notrump is not a frequent bid. With advancer holding a 5-card suit in the opening suit bid, a Notrump advance is a much less risky bid than any other alternative. Finally, after the opening lead, with the dummy laid open, the tally shows that EW have 8 sure winners, one less than required for their Notrump game bid. Declarer's only hope is to develop an extra trick. While the 3-notrump advance is the best bid to make game, making 9 tricks will be difficult and, in this scenario, the skill to make 9 tricks is beyond beginning bridge.*

CHAPTER 9

OPENING LEAD CARDS AND THE STRATEGY OF DEFENSE

SETTING THE STAGE FOR AN OPENING LEAD: THE FIRST PLAY IN THE PLAY OF THE TRICKS

The side that loses the auction becomes the defense and wins the right to make the **OPENING LEAD**, the first card played in the first trick of the play. The Opening Lead is always made by the Declarer's LHO. The right to lead the first trick is an important advantage, especially if the game is being played in Notrump. Why? Because the Opening Lead gets the first shot at making a run of tricks with no risk of being ruffed. Not so infrequently, the winner of the Auction sees his contract defeated by a run of tricks before his side has had a chance to play their first trick .*The Declarers, to succeed, always need to make more tricks than the defense; and, the higher the bidding, the fewer tricks the defense needs to make in order to defeat the contract.*

According to estimates found in bridge literature, almost half the fulfilled contracts could have been set if the defense had made the correct opening lead. While there is no single, perfect Opening Lead, this Chapter's mission is to present the strategy that helps the Beginner select the best available opening lead.

SELECT THE OPENING SUIT BEFORE SELECTING THE OPENING LEAD CARD

An opening lead consists of two ingredients: a card and a suit. Before the card can be selected, the opening suit must be identified. The following are some of the factors the Beginner should consider when selecting the opening suit:

- Select the suit your partner bid during the auction; he would not have bid it if it was not his best suit.

- Only if you think you have a longer or more powerful suit than what your partner bid, should you lead it.

- If partner has not bid, and the Play is in Notrump, prefer Long Suits headed by Touching Cards; and, if the contract is in a suit, prefer Short Suits with sequences in High Card winners that can be quickly voided, so that you can go on to your next Short Suit and repeat that same winning strategy.

- It is usually best to not select the suit that the other side has bid since that suit is presumably their longest and strongest suit and your holding in that suit is likely to be weak.

THE LANGUAGE OF SUITS, SEQUENCES AND CARDS

Once the opening suit is selected, the next step is the **CARDING DECISION,** selection of the Opening Lead card from within the Opening Leader's suit. In order to fully understand the skill set associated with a carding decision, it is helpful to have an understanding of the language of suit holdings. A common holding in a suit is the **SEQUENCE,** three or more cards of the same suit in *consecutive rank order. The* sequence can be all honors (AKQJ10); all spots (98765) or a combination thereof (J10987). **TOUCHING CARDS,** Sequences of Honor Cards are also known as **TOUCHING HONORS.**

When a suit, regardless of its length does not have a sequence anywhere within it, it is a **BROKEN SUIT** (A9642, AQ10, KJ832, 8642). A broken suit may be headed by an Honor or it may not. It also can be made up of all Honor cards, all spot cards or a combination thereof.

A 2-card suit is a **DOUBLETON** and can be a sequence (KQ) or not (KJ); a 3-card suit may have a 3-card sequence (AKQ) or have a 2-card suit sequence within it (AQJ) or a broken suit within it (AQ9).

In the end, suit selections are a rather simple process, primarily dependent on the opening leader's judgment and what he has learned from the Auction. On the other hand, the carding decision is more complex because it depends on where the card is within a suit *and whether the opening lead is being made to a Notrump contract or to a suit contract.* The Opening Lead gives partner a clue as to what other cards are held in the suit led as well as a signal for partner to play a specific card that could lead to a run of tricks. This advanced skill set is known as **SIGNALING** and, for that reason, its introduction is limited in *Beginning Bridge*.

THE RULE OF ELEVEN AND FOURTH BEST

When playing defense, a helpful strategy is the **RULE OF ELEVEN,** the oldest rule in bridge. This rule uses a simple mathematical formula*: if the "fourth highest" card is led from one hand then the number of cards capable of beating that card is equal to eleven minus the rank of the card led*. This rule is designed to help the opening leader's partner once the dummy becomes visible.

In the illustration below, we will examine a 4-hand, 1-suit Card Diagram used by the OEB as an illustration of the Rule of Eleven in which the spot 7 is the opening lead card and identified as the fourth highest in the suit led: since 11 minus 7 equals 4, there are 4 cards with sufficient rank capable of beating the spot 7. The card diagram shows the four hands of one suit as seen by the opening leader's partner (East).

Once East recognizes the spot 7 as the "fourth highest," he starts his analysis by reviewing the cards that are visible to him: the 3 cards in the dummy, the 4 cards in his hand and the spot 7 which was the opening lead. Since he has visibility of 8 cards, that means that 5-cards are not visible and, by deduction, they are the Q J 8 6 4. Of those 5 cards, only the Q J 8 are senior in rank to the spot 7. Therefore, the two remaining cards, the spots 6 and 4 are either held by the opening leader below the spot 7 or, they are held by the Declarer.

East has now accounted for all 5 cards that are hidden: the QJ8 held by West, the opening leader; and, the spots 64, with *ranks less than 7*. East now focuses on identifying the 4 cards capable of beating the spot 7: the King in the dummy and the A 10 9 in his hand. Since the 4 cards have been located in the dummy and East's hand, the declarer has *no card higher than the spot 7.*

The play of the tricks starts with partner making the opening lead with the spot 7. If declarer does not take the spot 7 with the dummy's King, East plays the spot 3 and takes the trick knowing that declarer cannot beat the spot 7. ***The following diagram is the deal as seen from the eyes of East, the opening leader's partner:***

```
                    DUMMY
                    K 5 2
    x x x 7 led                 A 10 9 3
                    DECLARER
```

The following is the full 13-card deal based on the deductions made above: there are only 5 cards that are not visible to East (Q J 8 6 4). The spots 6 and 4 are arbitrarily placed with the declarer; they could also have been placed with the opening leader, immediately following the spot 7:

```
                    DUMMY
                    K 5 2
    Q J 8 7                     A 10 9 3
                    DECLARER
                    6 4
```

The FOLLOWING play of the tricks in this suit would look like this, with EW taking all four tricks:

ROUND #	LDR	PLAY	NS	EW
Round # 1	W	7---2---3----4		X
Round # 2	W	8--- 5---9--- 6		X
Round # 3	E	A---D---J---K		X
Round # 4	E	10---D---Q---D		X

Note: The "D" signifies a discard, one not of the suit led. The suit led is not given since this is a one suit play

CONVENTION CARDS AND CONVENTION CARD OPENING LEADS

A **CONVENTION CARD** is a printed card listing commonly used Conventions. According to the OEB it is used by players in duplicate bridge to indicate to opponents the Conventions and special understandings used by a pair.. A special section is also included for Opening Leads which lists an array of suits ranging from 2-card to 5-card suits with the suggested lead card within the suit printed in **BOLD**. There are two separate lists of suggested **CARD LEADS:** one, for when the lead is versus a suit; and, one for when the lead is versus Notrump. The player is requested to circle the recommended card lead if the pair's choice for that lead is not the one listed in Bold. For example, some pairs play the second card of a doubleton and some the top of the doubleton. As shown below, the Convention Card Standard Opening Lead for a doubleton is the top as shown in Bold. The lists are as follows:

CARD LEADS VERSUS SUITS	CARD LEADS VERSUS NOTRUMP
X X	**X** X
X **X** X	X **X** X
A K **x**	A **K** J x
K Q x	A **J** T 9
Q J x	**K** Q J x
J T 9	**Q** J T x
K Q T 9	**J** T 9 x
X X **X** X	**X** X X X
X X **X** X X	X **X** X X X
T **9** x	A **Q** J x
K **J** T x	A **T** 9 x
K **T** 9 x	K **Q** T 9
Q **T** 9 x	Q **T** 9 x
	T 9 x

FOOTNOTES:

- While the suit lengths are the same in both columns, the standard opening lead is not necessarily the same. For example with **K**QT9, versus suits, the standard opening lead is the K; and, vs. Notrump with K**Q**T9 it is the Q. Also, note that in 4-card suits, versus suits, the standard opening lead is fourth best, while, versus Notrump, the standard is the top of the suit.

- For suits headed by an Ace, no suggested lead is indicated in Bold in the Convention Card, when versus suits. Modern Bridge guidance now leads the A from the AK sequence versus suits. Now, when you lead the K, partner knows you do not have the A but you usually have the Q. When versus Notrump, the standard Convention Card lead when the suit is A**K**JX is to lead the King.

- A lead of a singleton A, K or Q is not considered a winning strategy because honors should be preserved to take opposing Honors. If you lead a singleton, you have voided your hand of that suit and the hope is that you will be able to ruff the singleton's suit if the opportunity presents itself.

- Leading from a Doubleton should be avoided unless it consists of 2 touching Honors.

CHAPTER 9
QUIZ # 6

OPENING LEADS

SCENARIO: A series of Bidding Conversations are shown, some competitive and some non-competitive. The hand shown is the hand of the opening leader. Your challenge, as West the opening leader is to determine the opening lead, by explaining your rationale for making the suit and carding decision, and, most importantly, what you learned by listening to the auction. Note that the opening lead card is always underlined in the Card Diagram.

BIDDING SEQUENCE # 1:

	WEST	NORTH	EAST	SOUTH
				1-NT
	2-S	2-NT	Pass	3-NT
	Pass	Pass	Pass	

Opening Leader: West

A K Q J 10
K 6 4
9 7
6 5 4

Commentary # 1: West's opening lead is any one of the 5 Spade Honor Cards against Notrump. The suit selection is Spades for two reasons: Spades are the opening leader's longest and strongest suit; and, his partner did not mention a suit. Since play is in Notrump, you may play any one of the 5 Spade Honor cards and you will enjoy a 5-card run in Spades. *Lessons Learned: Declarers can only afford to lose 4 tricks. Since West is going to enjoy a 5-card run in Spades, the NS contract will be defeated regardless of the number of tricks they take after that. While Lady Luck is the main determinant in the EW victory, this is a great teaching hand because it shows that a side, even with the likely majority of power cannot hold back an opening run of tricks when play is in Notrump. Another lesson taught by this bidding sequence is that when the opponents interfere with your Notrump bidding sequence (as West did by overcalling in 2-spades) the Notrump bidders should be wary if they have no stoppers in that suit since that would indicate an inferior contract, as is the likely case in this Scenario.*

BIDDING SEQUENCE # 2:

	WEST	NORTH	EAST	SOUTH
				1-NT
	Pass	2-NT	3-S	3-NT
	Pass	Pass	Pass	

Opening Leader: West

J 6 5 3
3 2
A 2
7 5 4 3 2

Commentary # 2: Your opening lead is the Spade spot 3, fourth best from a broken sequence. The suit selection is Spades because it was mentioned by partner, signaling a 3-level overcall requiring opening strength and at least a good 5-card suit in Spades. The combined EW hand should have at least a 9-card suit in Spades. IF EW can manage a 5-card run, they can set the NS contract. *Lessons Learned: While the 4-card Spade suit, headed by a Jack and followed by 3 spots, is not specifically listed in the Convention Card as a lead, it is a 4-card suit, indicating length and the standard for a length lead is 4th best. By selecting Spades as the opening suit, you have a 9-card Spade suit in the combined hand. Since EW makes the opening lead, and the play is in Notrump, EW may come close to defeating the contract. The goal of the defense is to set the contract; and, if that is not possible, minimize the number of Overtricks that NS can make. Since NS went to game in Notrump, they have at least 25VPs, the majority of the power.*

CHAPTER 9
QUIZ # 6 CONTINUED

BIDDING SEQUENCE #3:

	WEST	NORTH	EAST	SOUTH
				PASS
	1-H	1-S	3-H	PASS
	4-H	PASS	PASS	PASS

Opening Leader: North

A K 10 7 6
Q 7 6 5
Void
Q J 4 2

Commentary # 3: North's opening lead is the Spade-Ace, versus a suit. Beginner should note that this Scenario departs from the usual practice of South making an opening bid. Since South's call was a pass, West takes the lead with a 1-heart opening bid. North challenges the opening bid with a 2-spade overcall, signaling a good 5-card suit and 13-17VPs. If North had the opening lead, he would have opened in 1-spade. East shows 4-card support for West's opening by making a 3-heart response signaling 4-card support and 6-10VPs. Following South's second pass, West identifies a 9-card fit in Hearts and goes to game with a final bid of 4-hearts, promising 10 tricks. In this Scenario, we only know that West's point-count is in the 13-21VP range. Since East shows only 6-10VPs, it is likely that West has maximum opening strength. West's final bid is the cue for his LHO, North to make the opening lead. North's suit selection is Spades, his longest and strongest. The Spade-Ace card opening lead selection card reflects Modern Bridge practice to lead the Ace from the AK. *Lessons Learned: Since EW are the Declarers, NS, the defenders, need to make 4 tricks in order to defeat the 4-heart contract. Once the opening lead is made, the Declarer's partner, East, visibly displays his dummy hand. This is the Declarer's first opportunity to study his combined hand and make a plan for fulfilling his contract, making overtricks, or minimizing penalties. Based on what we see at this point, Declarer should have the 9-card fit his partner promised. It appears that the opening leader may have a run of 2 tricks in Spade and that the Heart-Queen may take a trick. At this point, without seeing the rest of the cards, Declarer is perilously close to being set.*

CHAPTER 10

THE END-GAME: PLANNING OF THE PLAY AND THE PLAY OF THE TRICKS

The term "End-Game" refers to the two final bridge events: The **PLAN OF THE PLAY** defined by the *Official Encyclopedia of Bridge (OEB)* "as the mental process by which the Declarer decides how to use assets of the combined hand to fulfill the contract and develop overtricks, or minimize penalties." The **PLAY OF THE TRICKS** is the play of each player's 13 cards. Playing the tricks without a plan is like going out into the open sea without navigational skills: if you do not know how to get where you want to go, you will certainly never get there.

Everything you do in bridge, up to the Play, is simply foreplay. The play translates tricks into scores and scores into victory. *In the end, winning bridge is making all the tricks you have bid and more. As w*ill be discussed shortly in depth, the Play of the Tricks should always be preceded by the **PLAN OF THE PLAY,** arguably, the most difficult bridge skill for the beginner to acquire.

DECLARER PLAY

While the auction's winners become the "Declarers;" the losers win the right to play the Opening Lead card, a not insignificant advantage since it can start a run of tricks that could defeat the contract before the Declarer makes his first play. Immediately following the Opening Lead, the Declarer's partner lays down his 13 cards face-up in 4 vertical columns. At this point, **DECLARER PLAY** begins and Declarer assumes responsibility for the play of all 26 of the cards in his combined hand.

THE MECHANICS OF DECLARER PLAY

When the Opening Lead card has been played, the next card played is *from the dummy, with* the Declarer following the suit led. However, before the Declarer makes his selection, he takes a minute or two to mentally envision how to fulfill his contract, make Overtricks or minimize Penalties. This mental process is known as the Plan of the Play; and, it is understandable that beginners may be embarrassed into taking less time than they should, especially when playing with more skilled players. Try to fight that impulse and take the one or two minutes allotted to this essential task.

THE DECLARER'S PRIORITIES

One of the first tasks required of a Declarer, when almost simultaneously seeing the Opening Lead and the dummy hand is to determine if the Opening Lead will generate a serious run of tricks and if there is one, how it can be contained. Declarer's next priority, with the dummy now visible, is to perform the Declarer's Tally; the counting of **SURE WINNERS**, tricks that a player is more than likely to make, if led. It is that Tally that determines the extra needed tricks, if any to fulfill the contract. Frequently, a Declarer is not able to lead a Sure Winner when, for example, it is in the dummy and the lead is in the Declarer. In that instance, that Sure Winner cannot take a trick because it cannot be led.

When the Declarer has such difficulties, he is said to have a **COMMUNICATION** problem, *difficulty in transferring the lead from one hand to the opposite hand.* Sometimes, the opportunity to lead Sure Winners never materializes and they may become discards, never taking a trick. In Planning of the Play Scenario # 3 below, there is an excellent example of the Declarer solving his Communication Problem by leading a low card to the dummy and a High Card taking the trick, thereby transferring the lead from the Declarer to the dummy.

When the contract is in a trump suit, the Declarer also counts **SURE LOSERS;** cards which will more than likely lose a trick if led. In Scenario # 3, the Declarer disposes of Sure Losers by Discarding, trumping losers in dummy and following suit with a Sure Loser when the trick will be won by the other side.

While point-counts are important when estimating trick-taking potential, beginner should realize that these are only estimates since they are made before dummy becomes visible. The counting of Sure Winners is a much more precise method for determining a hand's trick-taking potential because they will take tricks, if they can be led.

If your tally shows more sure winners than you need, don't celebrate since you likely **UNDERBID** your hand, by underestimating its trick-raking strength. In a Rubber Scoring Format, only tricks bid *and* made count towards making a contract. So, if you bid 9 tricks and make 10 tricks, the 9 tricks count towards making the contract; and, the 10th trick counts as part of the Total Point-Score, but not towards making the contract. It is a Law of Contract Bridge that the only tricks that count for scoring purposes are those made above **BOOK,** the first 6 tricks made in the play; for example, with a 1-notrump final bid the contract requires 7 tricks. So, when only 7 tricks are made, only one trick counts for scoring purposes. The ultimate goal in a Rubber Scoring Format is the Total Point-Score (those counting towards game and those not counting towards game.) The best way to do that is to bid all the tricks you can make and make all the tricks you have bid.

When there are enough Sure Winners to fulfill the contract, it would appear that there is no need to Plan the Play other than to take your Winners as soon as possible. However, holding enough Sure Winners is not a guarantee that your contract will be fulfilled. For example, when play is in 1-notrump, Declarer can afford to lose 6 tricks and still make his contract. However, if play is in Notrump and the Opening Leader holds this 7-card suit: AKQJ1098, he can take 7 straight tricks before the Declarer gets to play his first Sure Winner. Also, when play is in a trump suit, holding just enough Sure Winners may still not get you to game: for example, **UNFAVORABLE** divides and Communication problems are two adverse situations, becoming apparent during the Play of the Tricks, preventing the fulfillment of contracts.

When the total Sure Winners in your hand are less than what is needed to fulfill the contract; a **DEFICIT** exists. Having a deficit does not mean that your contract is doomed; it only signals a need to identify the opportunities for developing those extra needed tricks. That process, which, when completed becomes The Planning of the Play, is one of the most important skill sets in a bridge player's repertoire.

There are a number of options available for the Declarer to develop extra needed tricks. This next section discusses at least five of those options, all within the range of beginning bridge players.

DEVELOPING EXTRA NEEDED TRICKS

TRUMP SUIT MANAGEMENT

Management of the trump suit refers to the skill with which Declarer utilizes the trumps in the combined hand; primarily, by mentally keeping track of all the trumps, whether they are with the Declarers or with the defense. When playing in a suit contract, trump cards are the Declarer's most valuable assets and have two important roles: drawing trumps from the enemy; and, ruffing the enemy's non-trump cards.

DRAWING TRUMPS FROM THE ENEMY

Drawing trumps from the enemy is a key strategy in Declarer Play. It is utilized by the Declarer to render the defense void of whatever trumps they hold. When the defense has been made void in trumps and the Declarers have trumps remaining, defense's ability to interfere with Declarer's play of the tricks is destroyed. Obviously, the more trumps remaining after the enemy is void, the greater is the Declarer's ability to interfere with defense's play. That is why an 8-card fit is better than a 7-card fit; why a 9-card fit is better than an 8-card fit; and, why a 13-card fit is better than any other fit.

There is little guidance in beginning bridge literature as to when the drawing of trumps should be initiated. There is guidance suggesting, for example, that launching Finesse should take precedence over drawing trumps because if Finesse fails there is time to develop an alternate strategy.

When the defense has been made void of their trumps, Declarers will want to keep some trumps in reserve while taking tricks with sure winners in their **SIDE SUITS,** suits other than trump suits, with interference by the defense..

Here's one way how to hold your remaining trumps in reserve: without a card of the suit led, you may discard**,** play any card not of the suit led; *stated another way, you are not required to trump a non-trump card that is led just because you hold trumps.*

KEEPING MENTAL TRACK OF TRUMPS

A fundamental skill in Declarer Play is **COUNTING,** the ability to mentally keep track of all 13 trumps. Once Declarer knows the number of trumps in his combined hand, he deduces the number held by the enemy; and, then mentally reduces that resultant total as the cards are played. When Declarer miscounts and continues to draw trumps after the defense is void, he seriously diminishes his ability to deploy trumps held in reserve. Although defense starts the Play with a certain number of trumps, some of those trumps may be played before the Declarer starts to draw trumps. So, when Declarer starts to draw trumps, he must know the number of remaining trumps the defense holds when he starts the draw.

Since 4 cards are played in a single trick, the most enemy trumps the Declarer can draw are two trumps per trick. For example, in this Scenario, when Declarer starts to draw trumps, Declarer hold 8 trumps that divide 5-3 and defense holds 5 trumps that divide 4-1; the trump suit will look like this when Declarer starts to draw trumps:

<pre>
                        DUMMY
                        J 10 9

        WEST   EAST
         2   6 5 4 3
                        DECLARER
                        A K Q 8 7
</pre>

The drawing of trumps is envisioned as follows in a 1-suit play diagram:

TRICK #	LDR	LEAD	SECOND	THIRD	FOURTH	EW	NS	REMAINING*
								5
01	S	A	2	9	3		X	3
02	S	K	D	10	4		X	2
03	S	Q	D	J	5		X	1
04	S	8	D	D	6		X	0

*"Remaining" column shows trump cards held by the defense at the start of the play and after each completed trick. Since the defense, in this Scenario starts with 5 trumps, that is the number of trumps that must be drawn to render them void of trumps. Defense's 4-1 divide is unfavorable because it requires the Declarer to use 7 of his 8 trumps to void the enemy's 5 trumps. Of course, Declarer is not aware of the unfavorable divide until the 4th trick is played and he has seen the defense's 5 trumps (65432) played out, at which point he knows defense is void of trumps.

An important fundamental of drawing trumps is that it costs you trumps draw those the enemy owns. The good news is that you also score tricks will drawing trumps. In the end, *happiness is voiding the enemy of their trumps while you end up holding trumps in reserve.*

Finally, Counting is not a skill restricted to drawing trumps; there are a number of situations when other suits are involved. This is a skill which beginner can use once he is able to deduce the distribution of hidden hands by listening to the bidding conversation or from information gained during the Play of the Tricks. While Drawing Trumps is an important option because it diminishes defense's ability to take tricks, it should not be launched simply because you have the opportunity to do so.

IDENTIFYING AND TRUMPING SURE LOSERS IN THE DUMMY

It is worth repeating that a Sure Loser is card that will usually lose a trick when led. Therefore, when the Declarer gets rid of a Sure Loser, he gets rid of the opportunity to lose a trick with that loser. One of the options for "making losers disappear" involves leading the Sure Loser to the dummy; and, then ruffing that loser with one of the dummy's trumps.

In order for this strategy to work, the play must be in a trump suit; the dummy must be void of the loser's suit or at least one trick away from being void; and, obviously there must be a trump available in the dummy. To illustrate this technique, we use the 2-hand card diagram shown in the Scenario presented below. Of course, before Declarer can trump a loser in the dummy, he must identify the suit and the loser that will be trumped.

SCENARIO: This is how the Declarer first sees his combined hand; with the visible dummy's suits arrayed vertically starting with the trump suit, Spades, on the left, followed by Hearts, Diamonds and clubs. The Declarer's hand is hidden and usually sorted in the same order, Spades, Hearts, Diamonds, Clubs. One of the Declarer's priorities is to identify his Sure Losers when the play is in a suit as well as the Sure Winners in the combined hand. That tally is shown below:

```
          DUMMY
          8  A  J  6
                5  6  10
             3  5  6
                2  5
                   4


          DECLARER
          A K Q J 10
          K 4 3
          K Q 2
          A 9
```

This Declarer's Tally includes the following Sure Winners and Sure Losers, the sum of which always add to 13

Spades:	5 sure winners	0 sure losers	
Hearts:	2 sure winners	1 sure loser (spot 3)	
Diamonds:	0 sure winners	1 sure loser (spot 2)	2 delayed winners (K Q)
Clubs	1 sure winner	1 sure loser (spot 9)	
Totals	8	3	2

Diamonds Zero Sure Winners does not mean that the KQ are Sure Losers. Rather, they are Delayed Winners who become Sure Winners, if led, once the Sacrifice Play (made with the Q J or 10) draws the Diamond-Ace and takes the trick. Note the sum total of sure winners, sure losers and delayed winners will always total 13.

Also, note that the dummy's 2 spades are not included in the count of the 5 Spade Sure Winners because every time one of the 5 Spade winners is played by the declarer, a dummy Spade must follow suit; thereby using 2 of the Declarer's Spades to make 1 trick. However, if one of the dummy's Spades can be played against a non-trump suit that the other side led, that Spade will win a trick. When that happens, there will be 6 tricks made with Spades, not 5. That result is exactly what "trumping losers in the dummy" accomplishes! This also is an example of when not to pull all the opponents' trumps before you have the opportunity to utilize one of the dummy's trumps to take care of a loser.

While there are various methods for developing extra needed tricks, Declarers will usually select the ones that are the easiest to make. For example, in order to trump a loser in the dummy, there either must be a void in the dummy or a suit in the dummy that is one trick away from becoming void. In the above Card Diagram, the suit closest to becoming a void in the dummy is the dummy's 1-card Club suit.

With the lead from his hand, Declarer leads the Club-Ace, a sure winner and wins the dummy's Club spot-6. Now, with the dummy void of Clubs and the lead still with Declarer, he leads the Club spot 9, a Sure Loser. Since the dummy is now void in Clubs, the Declarer can play any one of the 3 spot Spades that *originally were not included in the count of Spade Sure Winners* and any one of those spot Spades can defeat the Club spot-9 and take the trick. The net result is that one extra Sure Winner was developed in Spades. Trumping losers in the dummy is a beginning bridge skill that develops extra sure winners that can take tricks.

DISCARDING SURE LOSERS

In addition to trumping losers in the dummy, another way of disposing sure losers is the Discard**,** a card played to a trick which is neither of the suit led nor of the trump suit. Let's look at a 1-trick Play Diagram in which play is in Notrump:

TRICK#	LEADER	LEAD	SECOND	THIRD	FOURTH	EW	NS
01	W	C-Q	C-A	D-4	C-5		X

The lead is from West who plays the Club-Queen; followed by the Second Seat, North who plays the Club-Ace. At that point, since play is in Notrump it is certain that the trick will be won by North. East, in the third Seat, is void in Clubs and cannot follow suit. East's best option is to discard the Diamond spot-4, one of his sure losers. When the Fourth position plays his card, following the suit led, the trick is officially over and the winner of the tricks is NS. The net result is that East has eliminated a sure loser from his hand that would have lost a trick if led.

Discarding, is an advanced skill in which the player decides which cards to throw away and which cards to keep in the later stages of the play. When played by defenders, discards can convey information between themselves. When used in that manner, discarding is also known as Signaling**,** an advanced bridge skill, not part of beginning bridge. **Discarding sure losers can remove from the holder's hand a card that will lose a trick if led.**

DEVELOPING SURE WINNERS THROUGH PROMOTION AND LENGTH

Perhaps, the two most popular methods for developing extra needed tricks are from **PROMOTION,** driving out the *opponent's* higher ranking cards in that same suit; and, from **LENGTH,** by continuing to lead a suit until defenders have no cards left. Let's start with the Promotion strategy using the following four hands in a 1-suit Card Diagram in which both sides have likely divides:

```
                    DUMMY
                    K Q J
        WEST                    EAST
        A 9 8                   7 2
                    DECLARER
                    10 6 5 4 3
```

If you were performing the Declarer's Tally of Sure Winners, you would assign Zero Sure Winners to his suit's combined hand. The KQ in the dummy are Delayed Winners since they cannot take a trick until the other side's Ace is drawn out to take a trick.

The fact that the Declarer does not know in which hand the Ace resides does not prevent the promotion of the KQ into winners. What is required is the play of a card that is sufficiently high in rank to motivate the holder of the Ace to take the trick. Beginner should note that West, the holder of the Ace, in this deal, has visibility of the Dummy hand and is aware of what the Declarer is trying to do.

Let's see how Delayed Winners and other tricks are developed when the play is in Notrump and the lead is from the board:

Trick #	Leader	Lead	Second	Third	Fourth	EW	NS
01	N	J	2	3	A	X	
02	W	8	Q	7	4		X
03	N	K	D	5	9		X
04							

Note: the "D" in Trick # 3 represents a Discard, a card not of the suit led and not a trump suit.

After Trick # 01, the Declarer has promoted the KQ into winners by driving out the Ace who takes the trick. Now, there are two remaining cards, the 10 and spot-6 in the Declarer. Since EW is now void in this suit, the remaining two cards are Sure Winners, if led. In the end, Declarer's combined hand with Zero Sure Winners will take 4 tricks.

The only obstacle to these two remaining spots taking a trick is that Trick # 03 was won from the dummy and the two remaining cards are in the Declarer's hand. That is why the caveat, "if led" was added to their new Sure Winner status.

Since the lead is not from his hand, Declarer must wait for his "next opportunity" to lead from the dummy. Until that "next opportunity to lead" occurs, the Declarer endures what is known as a Communication Problem: when the Declarer is not able to transfer the lead to the dummy hand which made the last trick to his hand. One solution is to wait for the lead to come to the declarer so that he can cash the remaining two cards. Another option would be to play a spot from a different suit to a winner in that different suit in the dummy. When the winner takes that trick, the lead is now from the dummy and he can play the last 2 cards remaining. See Scenario # 3 below for an example of the Play.

In the end, NS will have made 4 tricks from a suit that originally had Zero sure winners; and of those 4 tricks, two were made from promotion (KQ) and two (10 and 6) were made through length because they were the last 2 remaining cards in the suit. While the strategy that promotes winners through length works best when the contract is in Notrump, it also applies, but with less success, when the contract is in a trump suit. Finally, when promoting winners through length, an 8-card or longer suit in the combined hand is preferred. Developing winners through Promotion and Length are beginner skills that work when play is in Notrump and in a Suit

EXTRA TRICKS THROUGH FINESSE

FINESSE develops extra tricks by trapping an opponent's High Cards when the enemy holds higher ranking High Cards that are favorably located. The one-suit, 4-hand Card Diagram show below sets the stage for Finesse, described as a "virtual" setting because in Real Bridge South would not have visibility of his opponents' hands. In fact, the essence of Finesse is making the Queen a winner when the Declarer does not know the location of the King, the one enemy card that can take the Queen.

```
                        DUMMY
                        Q 6 3
        WEST                            EAST
        K J 10 9                        8 7 2
                        DECLARER
                        A 5 4
```

The Declarer's combined NS hand holds only one sure winner, the Ace. When the Declarer needs to develop an extra trick, Finesse is an option which attempts to convert the Queen into a winner. Since the lead is with the Declarer, he takes the first trick with his Ace and leads the spot-4. Since the Ace has been played, West can take Trick # 02 without fear of being taken. Now, whatever card West plays in Trick #03, the Queen will take it and Finesse is successful. Let's look at Play Diagram that describes the play of this 1-suit 4-hand Card Diagram when the play is in Notrump and the lead is from the Declarer:

```
TRICK  LDR   LEAD   SECOND   THIRD   FOURTH        EW    NS
01     S     A      9        3       2                   X
02     S     4      K        6       7             X
03     W     10     Q        8       4                   X
```

If the original lead was from the dummy rather than the Declarer, the spot 3 would have been led to the Ace and the Declarer would take the trick with the Ace. Declarer would then lead with the spot 4 and West would then take that trick. With that, the Queen becomes a winner and the Finesse is successful.

SUMMARY OF OPTIONS FOR DEVELOPING EXTRA NEEDED TRICKS

As shown above, there are a number of ways for beginner to develop tricks when extra tricks are needed to fulfill the contract; or, to generate Overtricks: The following are the options available to the beginner for developing tricks:

- Trumping losers in the dummy;
- Discarding losers;
- Promoting winners by driving out the other side's higher ranking cards;
- Developing winners through length: by continuing to lead a suit until other side has no cards left.
- The Finesse, an option which only has a 50% chance of success

All these bridge skills are beginning bridge skills and can be used either in a suit or a Notrump contract, with the best results usually occurring when play is in Notrump.

TEACHING VIRTUAL BRIDGE VERSUS TEACHING REAL BRIDGE

We now reach that point in our beginning bridge journey when it is necessary to distinguish between Virtual and Real Bridge. In Virtual Bridge, whether the medium is a computer game, a classroom or, in this case, a book, the setting is inevitably *artificial*.

Up to this point in the beginner's journey, virtual settings are effective for teaching basic rules, Conventions and skills. However, that teaching method becomes less effective when it involves the End-Game: the Planning of the Play and the Play of the tricks. In both of these bridge events, it becomes increasingly difficult to re-create the Real Bridge environment, especially when the End-Game is involved.

So, while Virtual Bridge has served us well up to this point, we now must revise the teaching model to more realistically create the final steps in the beginning bridge journey, the End-Game.

GETTING FROM THE DEAL TO THE PLAN OF THE PLAY AND THE PLAY OF THE TRICKS

The OEB's definition of the Plan of the Play is worth repeating: "the mental process by which the Declarer decides how to use assets of the combined hand to fulfill the contract and develop overtricks, or minimize penalties." Beginner should note that Plan is not restricted to fulfilling the contract; it is also used to generate overtricks when they are available for development and to minimize Penalties as appropriate.

In the Rubber Scoring Format, the winning side is the one that has the highest Total Point-Score, points that count towards game as well as those that do not. So, when the Declarer is satisfied that he has the tricks to fulfill the contract, his next priority is to explore opportunities for making overtricks until no more are available..

In Real Bridge, there are four major **DATA POINT EVENTS,** data presentations that transport the Declarer to the point where he is able to Plan the Play. Those Data Point Events are as follows:

- The Opening Bidder values his hand so that he can make the Opening Bid.

- The Bidding Diagram of the Auction reports the Calls made and is known as the **BIDDING CONVERSATION,** providing important intelligence regarding the other side's holdings.

- The Opening Lead card from the Declarer's LHO provides clues about defense's strongest suit; as well as the potential to start a run which could be damaging to the Declarer. The Opening Lead is also the cue for the Declarer's partner to make the dummy visible.

- The Declarer's Analysis of his combined hand includes the Tally of the extra needed tricks, if any, to fulfill the contract; identifies Sure Losers when play is in a suit; makes deductions regarding the other side's holdings; and identifies suits that can yield extra tricks as well the most likely options that can deliver those tricks. It is the Declarer's Analysis that permits a formulation of the Plan of the Play and the Play of the Tricks which executes the Plan**.**

PLAN OF THE PLAY

More often than not, when the Declarer completes his Tally of Sure Winners, he will need extra tricks in order to fulfill his contract. The Plan of the Play determines that extra tricks are needed; identifies the suits which can provide those tricks; and, the options which can develop those tricks. This process is not possible until the Dummy becomes visible.

There is an axiom in naval strategy that states a battle plan lasts until its first encounter with the enemy. Similarly, in bridge, the Declarer frequently encounters in the Play of the Tricks unplanned adverse situations such as unfavorable divides and Communication Problems. For that reason, the Declarer's Plan of the Play should be flexible enough to encounter adversity and react appropriately in a timely manner.

While well formulated and flexible Plans frequently save contracts by developing extra needed tricks, even the most solid Plan cannot save a contract that is the product of poor bidding; promising more tricks than can reasonably be expected to be made or developed.

THE STRATEGY FOR THE PLAY OF THE TRICKS

The Plan of the Play is really the Declarer's plan for the Play of the Tricks. While opportunities for developing extra needed tricks are identified and formulated in the Plan of the Play, the actual making of those tricks happens (or doesn't happen) in the Play. Even when extra tricks are not required, the Play of the Tricks still requires a basic strategy. For example, when play is in a trump suit, it is a good strategy to determine when it is appropriate to draw the enemy's trumps. Simply because the drawing can be launched may not mean that the timing is right.

For example, Finesse should be played early on since it is only successful 50% of the time. When it fails, Declarer needs the flexibility to look for another source of tricks earlier rather than later. Similarly, when the Declarer discovers that the enemy's trumps have divided unfavorably, it may make sense for the Declarer to stop drawing trumps and start taking his sure winners from his side suits. This permits Declarer to keep some trumps in reserve for later use. Another common problem in Declarer Play is the Communication Problem, the inability to transfer the lead from one hand to the opposite hand. In that situation, the guidance is usually to play the desired lead at the next opportunity; or, better still avoid the problem by planning ahead so as to avoid, if possible, ending up in a position where your sure winners cannot be led. .

PLAY SCENARIOS AND TEACHING THE END-GAME

What follows now is the first of three Scenarios that will be employed to teach the beginner the End-Game of bridge: Planning of the Play and Playing of the tricks. Both of these events are performed by the Declarer who has only a limited time available to complete his analysis, formulate his Plan of the Play and start to play the tricks to determine if his assumptions resembled reality. .

With the above as background, we now present a protocol for teaching the beginner the skill needed to develop the Plan of the Play. We are using an approach that is as close to "Real Bridge" as is possible: by displaying what you will see and hear during each of the Data Point Events leading up to the Plan of the Play, including the sequence in which those events occur.

The teaching format includes three numbered Scenarios: for example in Scenario # 1, the Declarer's challenge is to develop an extra trick to fulfill his contract as well as to explore opportunities for Overtricks. In order to develop extra tricks, Declarer needs to identify suits likely to yield extra tricks and the options available to do that. Since a likely option is to Finesse, that becomes the title of the Scenario: "Lady Luck and the Finesse."

From this point on, we will attempt to deviate as little as possible from Real Bridge and only when it facilitates the learning experience. Our goal is to place the beginner into the mind of the Declarer whose priority is to ensure that his partnership fulfills their contract and make as many overtricks as are possible

THE PLANNING OF THE PLAY
SCENARIO # 1
LADY LUCK AND THE FINESSE

The four numbered **DATA POINT EVENTS** shown below are presented in the actual order of their appearance in Real Bridge: They contain all the raw data needed to perform the Declarer's Analysis which is the basis for the Plan of the Play and the Play of the tricks.

THE OPENING BIDDER'S HIDDEN HAND

A K 4
K 8 6
J 9 7 5
A Q 4

DATA POINT EVENT # 1 is the opening bidder's hand, sorted as shown above. The opening bidder was selected to be the dealer because he drew the highest card in the draw. His partner will be the player who draws the second highest card. This is an above average hand in terms of trick-taking potential: 17HCPs, in a perfectly balanced 4-3-3-3 shape. At this point, all four hands have been dealt and all four hands remained hidden..

THE AUCTION

WEST	NORTH	EAST	SOUTH
			1-NT
PASS	PASS	PASS	

DATA POINT EVENT # 2 includes the Bidding Diagram which records the Auction's Bidding Conversation from beginning to end. One of the Auction's prizes is the right to name the strain of the final bid because it allows the partnership to win the greatest number of tricks when played in that strain. Once the Auction is completed, the first player to mention the denomination of the final bid becomes the Declarer; and, his partner becomes the holder of the hidden dummy hand.

DECODING THE BIDDING CONVERSATION

This Auction is unusually non-competitive in that the only bidder was the Opening Bidder, who becomes the Declarer the final contract promising 7 tricks. Since the Opening Bid signals a limited holding of 15-17HCPs; and, since Responder did not bid, he cannot hold more than 7 points, making him too weak to make an invitational 2-notrump response. It would appear that both sides are relatively equal in strength. Since the opening was in 1-notrump, West would need a 2-level Overcall, requiring Opening Strength to be legal. In the end, without much bidding there is not much conversation to decode.

THE OPENING LEAD: SPADE 10 CARD FROM WEST

DATA POINT EVENT # 3 occurs when the Opening Lead is led face-up, immediately following the final pass in the Auction. The Opening Lead is also the cue for the dummy to make his hand visible. Declarer notes that his combined hand has a 6-card Spade suit and quickly deduces that defense has a 7-card suit in Spades. The Opening Lead is a significant event because it can start a run of tricks that can seriously jeopardize the Dealer's contract, especially when the play is in Notrump and the defense has a long suit in Spades.

With the Spade-10 as the opening lead, Declarer, holding the Spade AK could take 2 tricks; instead he plans to hold his Spade-Ace in reserve and only take Trick # 1, with the Spade-King. The lead is now with Declarer and the dummy is visibly displayed as follows:

```
   8    A    8    8
   5    Q    4    7
   2    5    3    5
                  3
```

Note the Dummy Hand is displayed as shown in 4 vertical columns with the suits in descending rank order. Since the play is in Notrump, the suits are arrayed in descending rank order starting with the Spade suit so that the Declarer, sitting opposite the dummy will see the Spade suit on his left.

This is the first time the Declarer sees his partner's hand. Since the Auction was completed without visibility of this hand, it may be a painful moment for the Declarer. In this case, the Declarer should not be unhappy with his partner since the guidance for the responder is to pass with 0-7VPs and play in a part-score. In any event, the partner's hand is what it is and he must do the best he can with the cards he has been dealt. *At this point, 27 cards are visible to the Declarer (13 in his hand, 13 in the visible dummy hand plus the opening lead card).*

DECLARER'S ANALYSIS

DATA POINT EVENT # 4 is the last Data Point Event and the most important because it provides the Declarer the opportunity to mentally absorb his combined hand, displayed below and previously displayed separately in Data Point Events # 1 and # 3. Once the combined hand becomes visible, the Declarer is now able to begin the End-Game starting with the Declarer's Analysis which prepares the Plan of the Play and the Play of the Tricks.

The combined hand shown below is presented just as the Declarer sees it in Real Bridge. The Declarer's Analysis is usually a challenge for the beginner, especially the first time he encounters it. There is only a minute or two that can be allotted to the Declarer for digesting the combined hand and developing the Plan of the Play: the mental process by which he decides how to use the assets of his combined hand to fulfill the contract, develop Overtricks and/or minimize penalties.

VISIBLE DUMMY

```
8     A     8     8
5     Q     4     7
2     5     3     5
                  3
```

HIDDEN DECLARER HAND

A K 4
K 8 6
J 9 7 5
A Q 4

Declarer's first priority is to deal with whatever threat the Opening Lead presents. Since that concern was initially dealt with in Data Point Event # 3, the Declarer's immediate priority becomes the Tally which determines if there are enough Sure Winners in his combined hand to fulfill the contract. Declarer mentally notes that, for as long as possible, he must make every attempt to stop the defense from gaining the lead because both sides have about the same strength and the side with the Lead has usually has an advantage over the side that is only following the suit led.

The Declarer's Tally is done on a suit-by-suit basis; while done mentally, it is presented visually to facilitate the learning process:

- Spades   2 sure winners in the AK
- Hearts   3 sure winners in the AKQ
- Diamonds   0 sure winners
- Clubs   1 sure winner in the A

Totals   6

Even though the final contract is in the lowest level bid permitted by the Law of Contract Bridge, there still remains a 1 trick deficit which must be eliminated if the contract is to be fulfilled. Declarer can only afford to lose 6 tricks. Declarer's strategy is to take the Opening Lead with the Spade King and not continue play in Spades. His priority now is to formulate the Plan of the Play which includes prioritizing the leads he will make in the Play.

PRIORITIZING THE PLAN OF THE PLAY

Since a 1-trick deficit still remains, the priority now is to identify suits that are the most likely donors of extra tricks and to identify the options that can be used to develop those tricks. Declarer quickly identifies the Clubs in his combined hand as a suit that provides an opportunity to attempt the Finesse, an option that only has a 50% chance of success. Accordingly, the Declarer decides that his first priority, as soon as he gains the lead in Trick # 2, is to attempt the Finesse and convert the Club Queen into a winner. The rationale for attempting the Finesse before drawing sure winners in the other suits is that, if the Finesse fails it is better to know about it sooner rather than later when there may not be any flexibility.

If the Declarer takes his 3 sure winners in Hearts before attempting the Finesse it is likely that he will lose more tricks than is necessary. After taking the opening lead in Trick # 1 with the Spade King, the Declarer still has the lead.

Before the Declarer can attempt Finesse, the guidance requires the lead to be from the dummy; which, after taking the Opening Lead is still with Declarer. This is a classic Communication Problem which the Declarer solves by identifying a suit that can be led by the Declarer and won by the dummy; that suit is the Heart suit.

Declarer leads his lowest card in Hearts, the spot-6, which he takes with the dummy's Heart-Queen. Now that he has solved his Communication Problem, the Declarer has the lead from the board and starts the Finesse by leading the Club spot-3 to the Declarer's Club-Queen, taking the trick and the Finesse attempt is successful. Declarer follows that trick by cashing his Club-Ace, his 4th trick.

SCORING SUMMARY: at this point, the Declarer has taken 4 consecutive tricks while still denying defense the lead.

While the above indicates that the Declarer "has taken" 4 tricks, it is more accurate to say that the Declarer has *identified 4 winners that are likely to take 4 tricks in the Play*. In the end, the only winners that count are those that take tricks in the Play.

In order for the beginner to envision the play of the Finesse in Clubs, the following is presented:

FINESSING THE CLUB QUEEN

With the Declarer holding the Club-AQ4, the Finesse's ability for developing an extra needed trick in Clubs is an option to be explored. The goal of Finesse is to develop Declarer's Club-Queen into a winner. When attempting a Finesse, the challenge is the enemy's King; the only card that can defeat the Declarer's Queen. As a result, Finesse is successful only if the King is favorably located; and, since the King can be in East or West, the chance of it being favorably located is only 50%. This is the Declarer's combined Club hand:

DUMMY
8 7 5 3

DECLARER
A Q 4

In order to envision the play of the Club suit, the Declarer first deduces the enemy's combined 6-card Club hand as KJ10962 which likely splits 4-2. Defense's 6 cards are arbitrarily located for play purposes into the West and East hands as shown below. Now, with a 4-hand Card Diagram the Declarer can envision the play of the Club suit. The guidance for executing Finesse with this hand is to lead the spot-3; a low card from the board toward the card the Declarer hopes will take a trick (the Queen).

DUMMY
8 7 5 3

WEST
J 9 6 2

EAST
K 10

DECLARER
A Q 4

From the enemy's viewpoint, the King's location in East is the least favorable one when the lead is from the dummy, because the Ace can be located either with the Declarer or with West. When the lead is from the board, East, in the Second Seat, with visibility of the Dummy, will have trouble protecting his King. Until he is sure of the Ace's location, he will likely hold back the King.

The following 1-suit, 4-hand play diagram in Clubs, with the lead, now from the board, records the play and the success or failure of Finesse:

TRICK #	LDR	LEAD	SECOND	THIRD	FOURTH	EW	NS
01	N	3	10	Q	6		X
02	S	A	9	5	K		X

In Trick # 01, the Declarer leads the Spot 3 from the board; the King **DUCKS** and the Queen safely takes the trick knowing there is no card in West that can take the Queen. In Trick # 02, the Declarer leads his Ace and learns that it is his lucky day because the King is in a doubleton, enabling him to also take the King as well as the trick. The Finesse not only successfully converted the Queen into a winner, but it permitted the Declarer to deny the lead to the defense. Since one of the 2 tricks was taken with a sure winner (Club Ace) the net gain is 1 trick. *After cashing the Club-Ace the Declarer will stop playing Clubs in order to continue denying defense the lead.*

Since the dummy became visible, the Declarer has mentally kept track of the 6 sure winners he started with and those that he developed along the way. Of the tricks taken, only the Club Queen was a Developed winner, not included in the count of Sure Winners. Since 3 sure winners have been played that means that there are 3 remaining sure winners: Since one of the Sure Winners, the Heart-Queen was played to solve the Communication Problem, there are 2 sure winners remaining in Hearts: the Heart-A and Heart-K. Also, the Spade-Ace which, has been kept in reserve since Trick # 1, is available. At this point the Declarer has identified enough winners to ensure the contract will be fulfilled.

DECLARER PLANS THE PLAY OF THE TRICKS

As discussed, part of the End-Game is the Declarer's formulation of the Plan of the Play. During the course of this Scenario, we have discussed various strategies the Declarer must consider before launching into the Play of the Tricks. For example, Finesse, because it is likely to fail 50% of the time, should be attempted before taking Sure Winners. Opening Leads are always a potential threat to the contract and should be immediately evaluated in terms of the amount of damage they can inflict. Finally, maintaining the lead is essential to the Declarer and he has taken the necessary steps to make that happen.

Suits that are identified as possible donors of extra tricks should be quickly identified as well as the options that can deliver those extra tricks. For example, is Finesse possible; can a Sure Loser be trumped in the dummy; can winners be developed by drawing out a higher card; and, when holding the longer suit in a divide, can a winner be developed though length. Declarer will need to answer all these questions in developing his Plan.

In the end, Declarer's plans can be foiled in the Play by any number of adverse situations. Even with the best of plans, planned outcomes may not be the outcomes achieved in the Play. For example, when plans rely on likely splits, reality may serve unlikely splits. In the end, the only winners that count are the winners that take tricks.

As opera lovers say, "it ain't over till the fat lady sings." In bridge, it ain't over until all 13 tricks have been played out.

Lessons Learned: While the Play is the final determinant, getting to the Play is equally important. The four Data Point Events include all the data necessary for the Declarer to prepare for the End-Game: the Plan of the Play and the Play of the Tricks. The Opening Bidder's hand sets the stage for the first Call in the Bidding Sequence. The Bidding Conversation reveals valuable information based on what was bid and what was not. The Opening Lead card represents information regarding defense's ability to set the Declarer's contract. Once the dummy becomes visible, the Declarer can determine the trick-taking strength of his combined hand and whether or not there are sufficient winners to fulfill the contract. Finally, the Declarer formulates the Plan of the Play: indicating how he will fulfill the contract by identifying suits that can yield extra tricks and options for taking those tricks.

The Play of the Tricks executes the Plan of the Play. Perhaps the most important lesson is that even the best of plans fail when the assumptions that form the basis of the plan do not reflect reality. While there are Sure Winners, Delayed Winners and winners that have been developed, the only winners that count are those that can take tricks.

Finally, Declarer's Analysis is a beginning bridge skill. while the "mental play" of the suits may seem beyond reach, that's a challenge the beginner can meet. The ability to mentally keep track of outstanding trumps or other winners is perhaps the most important bridge skill you can acquire.

Now that the beginner is accustomed to this "virtual bridge" format, there is less need for the author to intrude in the Declarer's mental formulation of the Plan of the Play and the Play of the Tricks. .

THE PLANNING OF THE PLAY
FLIRTING WITH THE LAW OF TOTAL TRICKS
SCENARIO # 2

DATA POINT EVENTS

THE OPENING BIDDER'S HAND

K Q 9 8 7
A 8
A 9 2
10 7 2

DATA POINT EVENT # 1 is the opening bidder's hand. Since this Balanced Hand does not meet the strength requirement for an opening in 1-notrump, the next priority is to open in a major suit, with: 13-21VPs and a 5-card or longer major suit. On that basis, this hand qualifies for an opening in 1-spade.

THE AUCTION

WEST	NORTH	EAST	SOUTH
			1-S
2-H	2-S	3-H	3-S
PASS	PASS	PASS	

DATA POINT EVENT # 2 above is the Bidding Diagram which reports the Calls made in this very competitive Auction, from start to finish. In this Scenario, the Bidding Sequence consisted of two Bidding Rounds with both sides competing. One of the prizes of the Auction is to name the strain of the final bid because it allows the winning partnership the greatest number of tricks when it can play in that strain. The winning bid, 3-spades, outbid the other side's final bid of 3-hearts. Since South was the first player to mention Spades he becomes the Declarer and his partner the dummy.

DECODING THE BIDDING CONVERSATION

This Auction is unusually competitive because both sides have opening strength and both sides made 3-level bids. Interestingly, neither side made a 4-level game bid, suggesting that both sides have about the same point-count and both are too weak to go to game.

Since the Bidding System is 5-card Majors, South's Opening signals at least a 5-card suit in Spades within a 13-21VP count range. West's 2-level Overcall signals at least a good 5-card suit in Hearts, within the 13-17VP range. North responds to partner's opening bid in 2-spades, signaling a weak 6-9VP point count range and 3-card Support for the Spade opening. If there were no interference from North, the raise to 2-spades would signal 6-10; but, with interference a 10+hand is reserved for a different bid, a cuebid. If partner had 4-card support he would have responded in 3-spades, identifying a 9-card fit in Spades. Since he did not, South understands that the 2-level response promises only 3-card support, identifying an 8-card fit.

Based on North's response, East cannot continue to compete in the Auction unless he raises the bidding to the 3-level, promising 9 tricks, which he proceeds to do. South now faces the same dilemma that faced East, he must go to the 3-level to remain competitive, which he does with a 3-spade final bid. At this point, both sides, based on the Bidding Conversation should be able to deduce that they both hold about the same number of HCPs. So, what's wrong with that?

Here's what the Law of Total Tricks' formula has to say about the bidding in this Scenario: the total number of trumps in the combined hands of both sides approximates the total number of tricks available on that deal. In this Scenario, the total number of tricks available in this deal is 16 (8 trumps in EW and 8 trumps in NS). So, when both sides have 8-card fits and 50% of the HCPs (about 20HCPs per side) each side could safely bid to the 2-level.

There are Scenarios with both sides only holding 8-card fits, where one side can bid well above the 2-level. For example, when one side holds 37HCPS and 8 trumps and the other side holds 3HCPs and 8 trumps, the side with the 37HCPS could make a 7-level bid, one that is well beyond the 2-level that the Law would consider safe with only an 8-card fit.

When, for example, the combined hands of both sides have about 50% of the HCPs and the longest trump fits are a 9-card suit on one side and a 7-card suit on the other side, the guidance permits the side with the longest trump fit to safely bid to the 3-level, promising 9 tricks and the side with the 7-card fit to safely bid to the 1-level, promising 7 tricks, an Imperfect Fit.

As previously discussed, the Law's formula is not infallible. The OEB warns that the accuracy of the Law's formula may be affected by extreme distributions, Queens and Jacks in the opponents' suits and double fits. That warning notwithstanding, the OEB endorses the Law as a "most useful bidding adjunct" in competitive auctions. Of course, the warning ceases to apply when players unsafely bid beyond the levels supported by the Law.

The next question, when applying the Law of Total Tricks is the Declarer's method for working out the total number of trumps in a side. Let's use the NS bidding conversation in this Scenario as example: South opened in 1-spade signaling at least a 5-card Spade suit; and, North's response in 2-spades signaled 3-card support. Based on that conversation, it is likely that NS has 8 trumps. Once the dummy becomes visible, the Declarer will know with certainty whether or not the combined hand has an 8-card trump fit. Of course, by that time the Auction is completed and no amount of bidding guidance can amend the final contract.

Determining NS's total number of trumps only solves half of the Law's formula; the Declarer also needs to work out the total number of trumps in the other side's combined hand. West's overcall signaled a good 5-card suit or longer. East's bid of 3-hearts, while competitive would require 9 tricks if it was the final bid. According to the Law's formula, East's 3-level bid is not considered safe. So, why would East deliberately break the Law of Total Tricks? .East may be thinking that the other side can make their 2-level contract and even if his side goes down at the 3-level, they are better off than letting the other side play safely at the 2-level. Further, his 3-level bid could also push the other side to the 3-level which may be higher than they could make.

Now, assume you are the Declarer and you want to use the Law's formula as a bidding guide: your interpretation of the bidding conversation makes you relatively certain that your combined side's total number of trumps is 8 trumps. East's 3-heart bid, if final, promises to make 9 tricks. As indicated above, it is also possible that East's 3-level bid is a Sacrifice Bid. Regardless of what East's 3-level bid means, it does not change the fact that the Declarer either must make at least a 3-spade bid to stay in the auction or he must pass. Since it is possible that Declarer's combined side only holds 8 trumps, the Law permits him to only safely bid to the 2-level. Accordingly, the Declarer should pass rather than bid unsafely to the 3-level. As the Bidding Diagram reports, South flirts with the Law of Total Tricks and rebids in 3-spades which becomes a final bid.

At this point, the bidding is completed and South must get on with the End-Game. All he can do is the best he can with the cards he is dealt and the bids he made. The Auction's final pass is the cue for the immediate play of the opening lead.

THE OPENING LEAD CARD, HEART-KING FROM WEST

DATA POINT EVENT # 3, the play of the Opening Lead card, usually signals defense's strongest suit as well as signaling partner that it wants the suit returned. The Opening Lead always has the opportunity to make a run of tricks which could seriously jeopardize the fulfillment of the Declarer's contract, especially if the play is in Notrump. In this Scenario, since the Declarer holds the Heart-Ace, he will take Trick # 1 as well as gain the lead for the next trick. Also, since Declarer's Heart suit is a doubleton, he is quickly voided, permitting him to use his Spade trumps against further Heart leads by the defense.

The fact that the Opening Lead suit is in Hearts is no surprise to the Declarer since West showed opening strength in Hearts in the Auction. According to the Convention Card, the King is the standard lead when the King is the top of KQx or KQT9 versus suits. The playing of the Opening Lead card is also the cue for the Declarer's partner to visibly display the dummy which is shown below:

```
A   7   K   J
6   6   8   9
3   3   6   4
            4
```

Since play is in trumps, the protocol is to array the dummy's suits in vertical columns, starting with the trump suit, Spades, so that the Declarer, sitting opposite the dummy will have the Spade suit on his left, with the other suits following in descending suit rank order.

Declarer mentally notes the dummy's 3-card Support of Spades and weak 8HCP hand, which should be no surprise since this is exactly what his partner's 2-level response signaled. Declarer also confirms his earlier observation that both sides are relatively equal from a point-count standpoint.

DECLARER'S ANALYSIS

DATA POINT EVENT #4 is the last Data Point Event and is very important because it provides the Declarer with an opportunity to mentally absorb his combined hand, previously displayed individually in Data Point Events #1 and #3.

VISIBLE DUMMY

```
A   7   K   J
6   6   8   9
3   3   6   4
            4
```

HIDDEN DECLARER HAND

```
K Q 9 8 7
A 8
A 9 2
10 7 2
```

This event is usually a challenge for the beginner, especially the first time he encounters it. For starters, there is only a minute or two that can be allotted to the Declarer for digesting the combined hand and, more importantly for developing the Plan of the Play: the mental process by which he decides how to use the assets of his combined hand to fulfill the contract, develop Overtricks and minimize penalties.

With so much to do, it is important for Declarer to prioritize his tasks; the first of which is to assess the potential immediate threat to his contract from the opening lead, the Heart-King. As discussed, since the Declarer holds the Heart-Ace, he will take Trick # 1 and will attempt to hold on to the lead for as long as possible.

Declarer's next priority is to learn if there is a trick deficit; and, if so, how he can eliminate it in order to fulfill the contract. That question is quickly answered by his Tally, performed on a suit-by-suit basis. In addition to counting Sure Winners, the protocol is to also count the Sure Losers when play is in a suit. Note that the Sure Winners plus the Sure Losers always add to 13. While this Tally is done mentally it is visually presented to facilitate the learning process:

- Spades   5 sure winners   0 sure losers
- Hearts   1 sure winner   1 sure loser (spot-8)
- Diamonds   2 sure winners   1 sure loser (spot 2)
- Clubs   <u>0</u> sure winners   <u>3</u> sure losers (spots 10, 7, 2)

Total   8   5

With 8 sure winners and a contract requiring 9 tricks, the Declarer has a 1-trick deficit. Since Declarer can afford to lose 4 tricks, while defense needs 5 tricks in order to set the contract.

With the dummy visible, Declarer knows that his 8-card Spades are the longest trump suit in his combined hand; however, in order to apply the Law's formula Declarer must work out the length of the longest trump suit in the combined hand of the defense. Since Declarer's Hearts in his combined hand are only a 5-card suit, he quickly deduces that defense's longest trump suit is an 8-card Heart suit. Therefore, the "total number of trumps" in the combined hands of both sides is 16. According to the Law's formula, the total number of trumps approximates the total number of tricks available on that deal. Simply applied, the Law suggests, in this Scenario, that either side could safely bid to the 8-trick level. At the same time, according to the Law neither can safely bid to the 3-level promising 9 tricks.

As previously discussed, the point-count system is not abandoned when using the Law; and, if one side holds 37HCPs and the other 3HCPs, the side with the 37HCP could bid to the 13 trick level, well above what the Law says could be bid safely with an 8-card trump fit.

In the course of this Chapter, we have encountered four different options for developing extra tricks:

- Trumping losers in the dummy
- Finesse
- Developing through Length
- Developing through Promotion (driving higher ranking cards out)
- Discarding Losers

Unfortunately, there is not an option that can repeal the Law of Total Tricks. Since the Law holds that there are a finite number of tricks, in a deal, it is not usually possible to develop more tricks, especially since the Declarer's combined hand only holds 20HCPs as well as 5 Sure Losers.

As previously discussed, a possible reason why East made his 3-level bid is that it was a Sacrifice Bid, a deliberate overbid to a contract that is not expected to **MAKE** in the hope that the penalty will be less than the value of the opponents' potential contract. As to why South made his 3-level bid, it is more difficult to find a rational explanation. Perhaps the intent of East's 3-level bid was to push the Declarer into bidding higher than he should have. In any case South made a 3-level final bid and he will have to play out his combined hand, likely going down probably one trick.

Lessons Learned: The OEB suggests that "a simple way to use the Law is to always bid to your side's number of trumps. It is a beginner skill to know when to use the Law of Total Tricks for determining the number of tricks that can reasonably be expected to be made; and, when not to use the Law, if the point-count supports a higher bid. In this Scenario, Declarer's estimated strength of his combined hand, before the dummy became visible, was at least 20VPs, not enough for a 3-level bid. With an overwhelming number of HCPs, the 3-spade final bid or even a game bid could have been made since the Law would not have applied. Unfortunately, for the Declarer, with only 20HCPs in the combined hand, this was not one of those times.

Finally, this Scenario was not designed to teach Sacrifice Bids in which a player purposely overbids because he loses fewer points by allowing the other side to win the Auction and the contract. To properly teach that skill, we would have had to expand the Scenario to consider a number of factors not presented in the Data Point Events that were provided: the relative scores of the two sides in the Rubber; the vulnerability of the sides; the factors that might have East encouraged East to not make a Penalty Double, etc. At some point, that expanded Scenario crosses the line and goes beyond beginning bridge.

APPENDIX TO SCENARIO # 2:

The beginner is encouraged, as a learning process, to Play out the 13 tricks in this full deal to answer one basic question: can South's 3-spade contract be fulfilled? To that end, we are providing the full deal which is based on the NS combined hand as known; and, the EW combined hand as deduced and arbitrarily distributed to the two defense hands based on likely splits. The full deal should look something like this with the play in Hearts and the opening lead as shown in the Play Diagram template shown below:

```
                        DUMMY
                        A 6 3
                        7 6 3
                        K 8 6 4
                        J 9 4
        WEST                            EAST
        10 4                            J 5 2
        K Q 10 9 5                      J 4 2
        10 5 3                          Q J 7
        A Q 3                           K 8 6 5
                        DECLARER
                        K Q 9 8 7
                        A 8
                        A 9 2
                        10 7 2
```

Should the beginner prefer to play the above full deal, the following blank Play Diagram is provided with the opening lead made by West, and with Spades as trump.

TRICK	LDR	LEAD	SECOND	THIRD	FOURTH	EW	NS
01	W	H-K					
02							
03							
04							
05							
06							
07							
08							
09							
10							
11							
12							
13							

THE PLANNING OF THE PLAY
SCENARIO # 3
THE STAYMAN

DATA POINT EVENTS

THE OPENING BIDDER'S HAND

```
          3 2
          A 10 9 8
          A K Q 5
          A 5 2
```

DATA POINT EVENT # 1 shows the opening bidder's strength (17HCPs), which determines the level of the opening bid; and, the hand's shape (balanced 4-4-3-2) which determines the strain of the opening bid, Notrump, in this scenario. With strength in the 15-17HCP range and at least 3 guarded suits, the hand is Suitable for Notrump. At this point, all four hands have been dealt and all four hands remain hidden.

THE AUCTION

WEST	NORTH	EAST	SOUTH
			1-NT
PASS	2-C	2-S	3-H
PASS	4-H	PASS	PASS
PASS			

DATA POINT EVENT # 2 is the Bidding Diagram which reports the Auction's Calls from beginning to end. One of the valued prizes of the Auction is the right to name the strain of the final contract; usually allowing the winning side the greatest number of tricks when it can play in that strain. South, the first bidder to mention Hearts, the final contract's strain, becomes the Declarer and his partner the dummy.

DECODING THE BIDDING CONVERSATION

While all the hands are hidden, the Bidding Conversation reveals important information about both sides. For example, the opening bid signals a balanced shape and a limited point-count range of 15-17HCPs. While the guidance is to *always open the bidding* in Notrump, if possible, the responder's priority is to get the side into a major suit contract with an 8-card fit because that will usually yield more tricks than play in Notrump.

To further that end, responder employs the 2-club Stayman Convention that basically says "I have at least 8 or more High Card Points and one or two 4-card majors; and, if you have a 4-card major that matches one of my 4-card majors, we have an 8-card major suit fit." (If the responder, even with zero points, had a 5-card Heart, suit he would have made a Transfer Bid in 2-diamonds instead of the Stayman.) When East follows the 2-club Stayman with an overcall in 2-spades, he promises a good 5-card or longer suit; 13-17VPs; and, signals interest in competing or, at least interfering with NS' bidding tempo.

When the Bidding Conversation reveals the length of an opponent's Spades, the Declarer is able to more precisely determine how his Spades will split than using the Probability Table. For example, in this Scenario Declarer, holding a 6-card Spade suit in his combined hand is able to quickly deduce that the other side has a 7-card Spade suit. Using the Probability Table indicates the likely split should be 4-3. However, by listening to the Bidding Conversation, Declarer will know that East holds at least a 5-card Spade suit and West likely holds a doubleton or singleton Spade, depending on whether the split is 5-2 or 6-1.

Because of East's 2-spade overcall, South responds to the Stayman in Hearts at the 3-level to be legal while ensuring that the side does not get too high. Responder's Stayman, signals at least 8HCPs which, when added to South's 17HCPs, reassures South that the side, with at least 25VPs is very close to game. Based on that point-count estimation, South bids 3-hearts, a highly Invitational Bid; signaling a 4-card suit in Hearts and inviting game if partner also holds a 4-card Heart suit. When North rebids in 4-hearts, he identifies the successful 4—4 card match in Hearts and the 8-card fit. With a final bid in 4-hearts, a game contract, requiring 10 tricks, is defined.

THE OPENING LEAD: SPADE-QUEEN FROM WEST

DATA POINT EVENT # 3 is the playing of the Opening Lead card, face-up, following the Auction's final pass. The selection of Opening Leads is based on guidance provided in Convention Cards, primarily used to indicate Conventions such as the 2-club Stayman or Transfer bids employed by competing pairs. The Convention Card also has a section on Leads; for example, the guidance for making the Queen the Standard Opening Lead is usually when the Queen is located at the top of a 3-card suit such as **Q**Jx, or at the top of a doubleton with **TOUCHING HONORS** such as **Q**J. When a suit has length, with 4-cards or more, the Opening Lead is usually the fourth best. For example, in Q7**5**32 the Standard Opening lead would be the spot-3, the fourth best card from the top, not the Queen. Note that the standard Opening Lead is always the card printed in bold.

The Opening Lead provides important clues as to defense's strongest suit. It is the job of the Opening Leader's partner, East, in this Scenario, to signal the best way to proceed. If partner likes the opening lead suit, he shows his interest by playing a High Card; or, if partner has no interest in the suit he can play a low card. This high/low method of signaling is known as "Attitude Signaling" and is a beginner skill.

Actually, East likes Spades very much, especially since he signaled in the Auction that he held a good 5-card Spade suit with Opening Strength. West's selection of Spades, therefore, should be no surprise since the guidance for selecting the Opening Lead suit is to bid the suit partner mentioned in the Auction, signaling that it is his strongest suit. Of course, if West had a more powerful suit, he would have led it.

This Data Point Event is also the cue for Declarer's partner to visibly display the dummy, arrayed as shown below. When play is in a trump suit, in this case Hearts, the trump suit is placed in the first column on the left FROM THE DECLARER'S VIEWPOINT. *Accordingly, the dummy's suits, in this Scenario are arrayed, as follows, from the left: Hearts, followed by Spades, Diamonds and Clubs.*

K	9	6	Q
Q	7	4	J
J	6		6
2	5		

Because of when it occurs, the Opening Lead's potential to make a serious run in tricks is the first challenge the Declarer must address. Declarer quickly deduces, with 6-card Spades in his combined hand (9765 in the dummy and 32 in his hand), that defense holds a 7-card Spade suit that based on the Bidding Conversation, must split 5-2 or 6-1. Recall East's 2-spade overcall which signaled at least a 5-card Spade suit.

East must recognize that the Spade-Queen could be a Doubleton or Singleton. For example, if the Declarer holds 3-card Spades, with East holding 5-card Spades and dummy showing 4-card spades, West's Queen could be a Singleton. In order to ensure at least 2 tricks in Spades, in that Scenario, East must overtake his partner's Opening Lead, the Spade-Queen. If East allows the Opening Leader, to take the first Spade trick, he might be foreclosed from possibly making at least a 2-card run in Spades. Accordingly, East overtakes the Queen with his King, takes a second trick with his Ace and leads his Spade-10 in an attempt to take a third trick in Spades. At that point, Declarer shows out in Spades and takes the Play's third trick with a low trump card from his hand.

DECLARER'S ANALYSIS

DATA POINT EVENT # 4 is the Declarer's Analysis, a review of all the data presented to him up to this point. For the first time the Declarer has an opportunity to mentally absorb his combined hand, displayed below in a format to facilitate the teaching process. It is worth repeating that the suit on the left-most column of the dummy's hand is always the trump suit, when play is in a suit.

The Declarer's hand, while hidden in Real Bridge, is displayed for teaching purposes as originally sorted, with the top row in Spades, followed by Hearts, Diamonds and Clubs. Of course, the Declarer is free to re-sort his hand in any manner he prefers and as often as he may want to do so, as long as the hand remains hidden.

VISIBLE DUMMY

K	9	6	Q
Q	7	4	J
J	6		6
2	5		

HIDDEN DECLARER HAND

3 2
A 10 9 8
A K Q 5
A 5 2

The Declarer's Analysis is usually a challenge for the beginner, especially the first time he encounters it. There is only a minute or two that can be allotted to Declarer for digesting the combined hand and developing the Plan of the Play: defined as the mental process by which the Declarer decides how he uses the assets of the combined hand to fulfill the contract, develop Overtricks and minimize Penalties.

The Declarer's first quick glance at the dummy is usually to see if there are any surprises. The dummy's 4-card Heart suit is no surprise since that is what the Stayman promised. On the other hand, the KQJ within the dummy's 4-card heart suit is a pleasant surprise. The dummy's Club-QJ6 suit indicates to the Declarer, who holds the Club-Ace that the Club-King is held by the defense and that a Finesse attempt in the Club suit may be appropriate. The dummy's 9HCPs when added to Declarer's 17HCPs indicates that there is enough strength in the combined hand to support the final bid of 4-hearts. From a bidding standpoint, there are no surprises.

After dealing with the threat posed by the Opening Lead in Spades, and his quick first glance at the combined hand, the Declarer focuses on extra needed tricks, if any, in order to avoid going down. As shown below, he only has 8 sure winners, which results in a 2-trick deficit. Declarer also knows that he cannot afford to lose more than 3 tricks. Since the Declarer expects to lose the first 2 tricks in Spades to the opening leader, he is perilously close to going down. With play in a suit, Declarer also identifies 5 Sure Losers, cards that represent tricks that could be lost to the other side if they are led. Declarer's plan will include how he intends to eliminate his Sure Losers as well as how he plans to develop 2 extra needed tricks.

The Declarer's Tally, while done mentally is presented on a suit-by-suit basis to facilitate the learning process as follows:

- Spades   0 sure winners   2 sure losers (spots 3, 2)
- Hearts   4 sure winners   0 sure losers
- Diamonds   3 sure winners   1 sure loser (spot-5)
- Clubs   <u>1</u> sure winner   <u>2</u> sure losers (spots 5, 2)

Totals   8   5

The Declarer reviews his options for developing extra tricks: through Promotion; through Length; and, through Finesse. The disposal of Sure Losers is also a priority for the Declarer since a loser that cannot be disposed of, must, of course, lose a trick to the opponents if led. Disposing of Sure Losers is usually by Discarding, the playing of a card which is not of the suit led, nor of the trump suit; following the lead with a loser when it is clear the other side will take the trick; and, the trumping of losers in the dummy. Since both the development of needed tricks and the disposal of losers occur during the Play, the Declarer's Analysis must determine how and when, in the Play, their execution takes place.

DECLARER'S ANALYSIS

IDENTIFYING SUIT DONORS FOR EXTRA TRICKS

With a 2-trick deficit, the Declarer's priority is to quickly identify suits that may be potential donors for those extra needed tricks and the options available for making tricks from those suits. Declarer initially identified Clubs as the suit in which to attempt Finesse. At that same time, Declarer, with an 8-card Heart suit in his combined hand versus EW's 5-card Hearts in their combined hand, notes the possibility of developing through Length an extra trick in Hearts. Finally, Declarer identifies a valuable asset, the Diamond side suit with 3 sure winners and 1 sure loser..

IDENTIFYING AND ELIMINATING SURE LOSERS

While the emphasis is on developing extra needed tricks to fulfill the contract, the Declarer is also mindful of the 5 sure losers that could represent tricks lost to the defense if they are not eliminated. To that end, Declarer notes that at least the first 2 tricks will likely be led in Spades by the defense, representing an opportunity to eliminate by following suit with his 2 Spade sure losers (the spots-3 2).

MAPPING OUT THE PLAN OF THE PLAY

Let's start mapping out the Plan by investigating the Club suit since it is the likely suit in which the Declarer will attempt a Finesse that converts the Club Queen into a winner. With the Club-Queen in the dummy, the Club-Ace with the Declarer and the Club-King with the defense, Clubs appear to meet the guidance for pursuing the Finesse option. As to when the Finesse option is executed, the guidance is to attempt it as early a possible. The rationale for giving it that priority is based on the reality that Finesse is only successful 50% of the time; and, if it fails, it is better to know it sooner rather than later in the play, when there may not be much flexibility remaining to revise the strategy.

FINESSING THE CLUB SUIT

The Finesse's "magic" is its ability, at least 50% of the time, to develop winners with High Cards when the defender holds higher ranking High Cards; as, for example, when Declarer has the Queen (a High Card but not a sure winner) and the defense holds the King (a High Card ranking higher than the Queen). Finesse is successful only if the King is favorably located, relative to the Declarer's combined hand. This is the Declarer's 6-card Club suit in his combined hand, as he first sees it when dummy becomes visible. As previously noted, before Finesse is executed there is only 1 sure winner in Declarer's Clubs, the Club-Ace:

DUMMY
Q J 6

DECLARER
A 5 2

As discussed, the only card held by the defense that can defeat the Queen is the King, which is held either in East or West; and, the only card that can take the King is the Ace, held by the Declarer. In order to envision the play of the Club suit, the other side's 7-card suit is deduced to be the K1098743. Since the Bidding Conversation provided no clues regarding EW's Clubs, the Probability Table indicates the likely split to be 4-3. In order to envision the playing of the Club suit, EW's 7-card suit is arbitrarily assigned as follows: 10843 in West and K97 in East. With those assignments made, we now can present one version of what the 13 Clubs could look like within a 4-hand, 1-suit Card Diagram:

DUMMY
Q J 6

WEST   EAST
10 8 4 3   K 9 7

DECLARER
A 5 2

When the lead is from the dummy, the Jack together with the Queen is what makes Finesse successful. When you lead the Queen and East follows with the King, Declarer takes the trick with the Ace, permitting the Jack to take the next trick, making the Finesse successful.

USING THE HEART SUIT TO TRANSFER THE LEAD TO THE DUMMY

In order for the Club suit to play out, the Finesse must be launched from the dummy. Since the lead is with the Declarer, he must transfer the lead from his hand to the dummy. Declarer solves this Communication Problem by leading a low card in Hearts to the dummy and taking the trick with the dummy's Heart-Queen. That play is shown as follows:

TRICK	LDR	LEAD	SECOND	THIRD	FOURTH	EW	NS
01	S	H-9	H-4	H-Q	H-3		X

PLAYING THE FINESSE

The Declarer now leads the Club-Queen from the board and the Finesse is launched. The following is how the Declarer envisions the play of the Club suit in the Finesse:

TRICK	LDR	LEAD	SECOND	THIRD	FOURTH	EW	NS
01	N	Q	7	2	3		X

When West does not take the first trick with the Ace, East learns that the Ace is with the Declarer since West would have taken the Queen if he held it. With Finesse successfully converting the Queen into a winner, there is no reason for Declarer to continue to play Clubs. Actually, a higher priority for Declarer is to now draw trumps. Finally, note that the 3rd sure loser, the Club spot-2, was eliminated in the first trick of the Finesse.

MINING THE REMAINING HEART SUIT WHILE DRAWING TRUMPS

Drawing trumps in order to void the other side of their trump cards is a basic strategy that eliminates the defense's ability to interfere with the Declarer's play. Since drawing trumps also generates tricks, the Heart suit is also identified as a donor.

The guidance as to when trumps should be drawn is somewhat vague in the literature of beginning bridge. The best advice this beginner has heard is that it should be done when there is no reason not to. Once the run in Spades was stopped, the Communication Problem was solved and the Finesse was successfully completed, it seems to be an appropriate time to draw the defense's trumps. With the other side void in trumps, there is no interference with the Declarer's remaining trick-taking. For example, an essential part of the Declarer's Plan is the taking of the 3 sure winners in the Diamond side suit. If EW is void of trumps, they will not be able to interfere with that portion of the Plan.

Hearts were initially identified by the Declarer as a suit with 4 sure winners in an 8-card suit within his combined hand. Let's look at the remaining Hearts, as they are now distributed in the 4 hands:

```
                  DUMMY
                  K J 2
        WEST               EAST
        6 5                7
                DECLARER
                A 10
```

Note: The original 13 card Heart suit was the K Q J 2 suit in the dummy; the Declarer held the A 10 9 8 suit; and, West held spots 6 5 4 while East held the 7 3.

DRAWING TRUMPS

With the lead still from the Declarer, the following play diagram shows the envisioned voiding of EW's remaining 3 trumps:

TRICK	LDR	LEAD	SECOND	THIRD	FOURTH	EW	NS
01	S	H-2	H-7	H-10	H-5		X
.02	N	H-A	H-6	H-J	D-2		X

EW is now void of trumps and NS holds the last remaining trump, the Heart-King, which, since it is a trump card will take a trick whenever it is played. Now, Hearts initially identified to have 4 sure winners will ultimately take 5 tricks because one trick was developed through Length when the Declarer continued to lead the suit until the other side had no Hearts left.

MINING THE DIAMOND SUIT

The Diamond suit was identified by the Declarer as a valuable side suit when he first glanced at his combined hand and identified the 3 Sure Winners, the A K Q. With the lead still with the Declarer and the enemy void in trumps, he is free to draw his 3 Diamond Sure Winners from his side suit without interference. At that point the Declarer has taken 5 tricks and with the 3 Diamond Sure winners, the Declarer needs 2 more tricks to fulfill his contract.
while the defense has taken 2 tricks.

ENDING THE PLAY

At this point, with three tricks remaining to be played, Declarer has enough Sure Winners to at least fulfill the contract

PLANNING OF THE PLAY

To return to the End-Game, Declarer formulated the Plan of the Play with a goal of eliminating the 2-trick deficit as follows: contain the 2-trick Spade run initiated by the Opening Leader's partner; transfer the lead from the Declarer to the dummy to set up the successful Finesse in Clubs; draw Hearts so as to render the other side void of trumps and, in the process, develop an extra winner through Length; and, once the enemy was void in trumps, draw the 3 sure winners from the Diamond side suit without interference. Declarer's plan succeeded because the Finesse converted the Club-Queen into a winner; a 5th Heart winner was developed through length; and, the original 8 sure winners took 8 tricks. Not insignificantly, at least 4 of the 5 sure losers were disposed of during the Play without losing a trick in the process.

EXECUTING THE PLAN OF THE PLAY

In the end, the Declarer's Plan of the Play is only a plan. The final result can only be determined by the full deal Play of the Trucks. All too frequently, Lady Luck can create adverse situations which can foil the best laid plans. For example, the Finesse could have failed if the King was in West rather than in East; and, if Declarer's Spades were a 3-card suit, defense's run could have taken 3 tricks. Also, when Lady Luck does not create an adverse situation, trick playing errors by the Declarer can subvert what was a good plan.

Many beginning players attribute trick playing errors to an absence of **CARD SENSE,** defined in the OEB as a "special aptitude for playing cards." Beginners should not waste time and energy worrying about whether or not card sense is in your DNA; Instead, emulate advanced players: **play frequently, avoid making the same mistakes, only count the important cards and always keep focused on the Plan of the Play.**

DECLARER'S ANALYSIS IS A BEGINNER'S SKILL

For the beginner, the envisioning and "mental play" of the Club and Heart suits in this Scenario may appear to be beyond their reach. Beginners should never forget that Intermediate and Advanced players were once beginners who confronted the same challenges and now routinely perform that bridge skill.

As shown in this Scenario and the previous ones, there is a process which the beginner must follow to simply get himself to the End-Game: exercise good hand valuation and bidding skills so that the final contract reflects the strength that is actually in the hands of the winning bidders; understanding the potential threat to a contract that the opening lead can represent; decoding the Bidding Conversation for information on the strength of the defense; deducing the make-up of the defense's suits once the dummy is visible; determining the trick deficit that needs to be eliminated in order to fulfill the contract; determining which suits are the most likely sources of extra tricks, mentally determining likely splits based on clues from the Bidding Conversation and the Probability Table; mentally envisioning the play of a single suit; and, finally, prioritizing strategies prior to the Play.

While all this may seem formidable, players, who once were beginners, do just that on a routine basis.

CHAPTER 11

SCORING FORMATS, VULNERABILITIES, DOUBLING AND TRADEOFFS

If you have made it this far, you must be enjoying bridge sufficiently to want to see how well you are doing against the other side. To that end, **SCORING**, the tallying of points earned in an event, is what enables you to determine who won and by how much. Further, by assigning a monetary value to the points earned, Scoring adds spice to your bridge life Since Scoring is a skill normally required at the end of the Play, there was some rationale for delaying its introduction until this point in the bridge journey. However, Scoring impacts your bridge strategy even before the Play; for example during the Auction when a risk-reward Trade-Off Analysis is made to determine how aggressive you can be in your bidding; and, if you decide to make a Sacrifice Bid how many tricks you can afford to go down.

RUBBER SCORING FORMATS

SCORING FORMATS are guidelines for scoring; and, they vary depending on the form of bridge you are playing. Since Enjoy Beginning Bridge is primarily limited to Contract Social Bridge, we present the **RUBBER SCORING FORMAT** based on the best of three games. When a **RUBBER** is won with a score of 2-0 you earn 700 **RUBBER BONUS POINTS**; however, if you win a Rubber 2-1, you only win 500 Rubber Bonus Points. There is no need to memorize the various point awards since whenever you are Scoring an event you are permitted to openly consult a **SCORING TABLE** in order to match Scoring Events with the points that are awarded when successfully executing those Events.

SCORING EVENTS

SCORING EVENTS are those which result in a score of one kind or another. The narrative below describes the various Scoring Events that may be encountered in the course of a Rubber. For example, winning a game in a Rubber is a Scoring Event in which at least 100+TSPs need to be scored in order to win a game. The number of TSPs needed to win a game depends on whether the final contract is in Notrump, a major or in a minor; and, the needed TSPs are 100, 120 and 100 respectively.

CATEGORIES OF POINTS

In a Rubber Scoring Format there are three categories of points: the TSPs, which are the points that count towards game; the **PREMIUM POINTS** which are made up of Bonuses for winning 2 games in a Rubber, Bonuses for making Overtricks, tricks made in excess of the contract; the Insult Bonus for making a contract that was Doubled for Penalty; and, the Honors Bonus for holding specified Aces and Honors; and, the final category, **PENALTY POINTS** awarded to the defense for each trick by which the Declarer falls short of the points required by the contract.

VULNERABILITY

The amount scored is not only dependent on the Scoring Event. For example, when a side wins a game in a Rubber, it becomes Vulnerable for the remainder of the Rubber. Vulnerability, from a Scoring context, means that, while the side is Vulnerable the values of Premium Points and the severity of Penalty Points are greatly increased. When a side is Non-Vulnerable, it enjoys "Favorable Vulnerability" because it may take advantage of the Vulnerable side's need for caution. When Vulnerable, a side may be more inclined to bid low-level contracts and less inclined to make Preemptive Bids. At the same time, sides that are Vulnerable are awarded larger bonuses for making or defeating contracts.

DOUBLED FOR PENALTY

In addition to Scoring Events and Vulnerability, the amount scored is also affected when their contracts have been Doubled for Penalty by the other side. When a contract is defeated Penalty Points are awarded to the defense for each trick by which the Declarer falls short of the contract. Those tricks are known as **UNDERTRICKS.** When scoring Undertricks, the amounts awarded to the defense are based on whether or not the Declarer is Vulnerable and whether or not the contract is Doubled.

MAKING MORE TRICKS THAN YOU BID

Making more tricks than what were bid is another Scoring event. In that instance, **OVERTRICK POINTS** are Bonus Points awarded to the Declarer for each trick made in excess of what the contract required. The Overtrick Bonus is based on Vulnerability and whether the contract is doubled or undoubled.

MAKING A CONTRACT THAT WAS DOUBLED FOR PENALTY

This Scoring Event is known as the **INSULT BONUS** and points are awarded for making a Doubled Part-Score or game contract, referred to as "50 for the insult." There are no Bonus Points for making a part-score contract in a Rubber Scoring Format.

HONORS BONUS

This Scoring Event is based purely on luck. Honors Bonus points are awarded when a player holds four of the five honors in the trump suit; all five honors in the trump suit; and, when all four Aces are held in one hand in a Notrump contract. The only skill involved in earning this Bonus is the "skill" of remembering to make sure it is scored.

SLAM BONUS

Making one of the two Slams is a huge Scoring Event. Slams must be *bid-and-made* in order to be scored. The points awarded for Slam Bonuses depend on the type of Slam-bid and-made and the side's Vulnerability. If a Doubled Slam contract is made, Declarer earns 50 points "for the insult."

Scoring Tables are presented below for each of the Scoring Events in which points are scored:

SCORING TABLES

TRICK-SCORE POINT TABLE FOR CONTRACTS BID AND MADE

WHEN CONTRACT IS IN A	MAJOR	MINOR	NOTRUMP
FOR FIRST TRICK OVER BOOK			
Undoubled	30	20	40
Doubled	60	40	80
SUBSEQUENT TRICKS			
Undoubled	30	20	30
Doubled	60	40	60

TRICK-SCORE POINTS are scored for tricks bid-and-made over Book (the first 6 tricks in the play) and are based on the strains as shown above. For example, an undoubled 3-notrump contract requires 9 tricks for the contract to be fulfilled. When the undoubled Notrump contract is fulfilled, the 7th, 8th and 9th tricks are scored based on the strains as shown above (Trick #7 earns 40TSPs since it is the first trick made over Book., and Tricks #8 & #9 earn 30 each for a total of 100). Any tricks made in excess of the contract are considered Overtricks and are scored separately.

THE RUBBER SCORE CARD

In a Rubber Scoring Format, all points counting towards game are recorded **BELOW THE LINE (BTL)** on the Rubber Score Card while all other tricks are recorded **ABOVE THE LINE (ATL)**. A sample Score Card is provided at the end of this Chapter as Figure # 2. The sum of the scores made below and above-the-line add to the **TOTAL POINT-SCORE.** In the end, the side with the highest Total Point-Score wins.

UNDERTRICK POINT TABLE FOR PENALTY POINTS AWARDED TO THE DEFENSE

	NON-VULNERABLE		VULNERABLE	
	UNDOUBLED	DOUBLED	UNDOUBLED	DOUBLED
1 Undertrick	50	100	100	200
2 Undertricks	100	300	200	500
3 Undertricks	150	500	300	800
4 Undertricks	200	800	400	1100
All others	250	1100	500	1400

Each trick the Declarer falls short of the contract is an Undertrick resulting in a Penalty Point awarded to the defense. In "Bridge-Speak, when a side, for example, makes 2 less tricks than the contract requires, it is said to "go down two." Undertricks are scored ATL. The lesson learned from the above table is that bidding more tricks than what you can make comes with a high price, especially when the contract is doubled and the side is Vulnerable. For example, the penalty point cost for going down 4 tricks when Vulnerable and doubled is 1100 points as compared to a Grand Slam bonus of 1000 points when Non-Vulnerable.

OVERTRICK BONUS TABLE FOR POINTS AWARDED THE DECLARER

	NON-VULNERABLE	VULNERABLE
For each overtrick		
Undoubled	Trick Score	Trick Score
Doubled	100	200

Overtrick Points are awarded for each trick made in excess of the contract. For example, if the contract is in 3-Notrump, the side needs to make 9 tricks. If the side actually makes 10 tricks, an Overtrick , a trick made in excess of the contract, has been generated. If the side is Non-Vulnerable and the contract is Undoubled, that is, not Doubled for Penalty, the Overtrick yields a score of 30TSPs scored ATL. The 30TSPs are based on the Trick-Score Point Table presented above.

Of course, at the same time that the Overtrick is being scored ATL, 100TSPs are being scored BTL and a game in Notrump has been made. The Total Point-Score for the Declarers is 130TSPs.

SLAM BONUS TABLE

SLAMS, contracts at the 6-level and 7-level, earn the following Slam Bonus points when they bid-and-make their Slams as follows:

	NON-VULNERABLE	VULNERABLE
Small Slam (12 tricks)	500	750
Grand Slam (13 tricks)	1000	1500

If a doubled Slam contract is made the declarer earns an additional 50 points "for the insult."

RUBBER BONUS POINT TABLE

RUBBER BONUS POINTS, earned by the first side to win two games: 500 trick-score points if the score was 2-1; and 700 points if the score was 2-0.

INSULT BONUS

A bonus of 50 TSPs is awarded for making any doubled contract, Slam, Game or Part-Score. (Note there is no Bonus for making a part-score contract in Contract Bridge's Rubber Scoring Format.

GAME BID TABLE

GAME BIDS, contracts at the 3-level, 4-level or 5-level for Notrump, major suit and minor suit contracts, respectively, earn the following trick-score points bid and made and are scored below the line as follows:

STRAIN PLAYED	TRICKS REQUIRED	TSPs EARNED	
		UNDBLD	DBLD
Notrump	9	100	200
Major	10	120	240
Minor	11	100	200

Note that Vulnerability is not a consideration when scoring a game bid in a Rubber Scoring Format. When a game contract is doubled and made, there is an additional 50 Bonus Points for making a doubled contract. This Bonus is known as the Insult Bonus.

PART-SCORE CONTRACTS are contracts made at levels not high enough for game. For example, a 2-level final contract in Notrump requiring 8 tricks is a Part-Score Contract since it is one trick less than what is required for game. When a Part-Score contract is fulfilled, it is recorded below the line; if the side can record another Part-Score in the next deal that now totals 100TSPs, or more, they can Score a game. However, if the other side makes game after the first Part-Score was recorded, then that score is "wiped out" in terms of counting towards the next game. The part-score, however, will count towards the final settlement in terms of total points scored made both below and above the line.

DOUBLING FOR PENALTY

When a defender is confident that the Declarer cannot make the number of tricks required by the contract, a Double for Penalty bid may be made after what is considered to be the last bid. That bid has a major impact on the final score when a contract is defeated because an Undertrick is Scored for the defense for each trick which falls short of the contract For example, if a side goes down 4 tricks Doubled and Vulnerable, 1100 Bonus Points are awarded to the Defense. Of course, if the Declarer makes the Doubled contract, his TSPs are twice the scores earned as well as earning the Insult Bonus of 50 points.

Since the Double for Penalty and the Double for Takeout are both verbalized in the auction as "Double," there is a possibility for confusion. The difference between the two is that the Takeout Double is made immediately following a suit opening and the Double for Penalty is made after a final bid has been made. Finally, a Double made immediately after a 1-notrump or 2-notrump opening can only be a Double for Penalty.

GUIDANCE FOR BIDDING A PENALTY DOUBLE

The original purpose of the Double for Penalty is to discourage the "Hand Hog" a player who goes out of his way to be the Declarer in as many hands as possible, usually by bidding in notrump. The penalty double is not seen very often in beginning bridge circles for two reasons: beginners do not tend to be "Hand Hogs;" and, in serious bridge play, it requires advanced bridge skills to determine when it is *very* unlikely that the other side will make their contract. Guidance suggests that a Penalty Double should not be made if the margin of victory is less than two tricks. How to calculate that "margin of victory" is what makes Doubling for Penalty a skill beyond beginning bridge. That should not be interpreted as meaning that the beginner will not be Doubled for Penalty in the course of playing a Rubber. For that reason, beginner should know its scoring implications.

THE MECHANICS OF THE SCORE CARD

A sample Rubber Score Card is attached as Figure # 3, depicting a tally of a 10-deal Rubber that was won 2-1. The Card has two lines preprinted in bold: the vertical line separates the TSPs scored for each side, always identified as WE to the left of the vertical line and THEY to the right of the vertical line; and, the horizontal line preprinted in bold, which separates those points scored **ATL** and **BTL.** When making the final settlement, immediately following the winning of the second or third game in the Rubber, all scored points are counted regardless of their position above or below the line. The winner is determined by subtracting the lower side's Total Point-Score from the higher side's Total Point-Score and the resultant is the amount of points by which the higher scoring side won. At a penny a point, do not plan on quitting your day job.

THE IMPACT OF SCORING ON BRIDGE STRATEGY

The ability to sort through all the transactions in all the plays and emerge with an accurate score that quantifies the difference between sides is a valuable bridge skill. Beginners are encouraged to become proficient in bridge scoring for two reasons: bidding effectiveness is enhanced when the scoring process is part of the strategy; and, to ensure that their victories and defeats are accurately recorded. The good news is that you will now learn how to score in a Rubber bridge format. The bad news is that you will be asked to be the scorer. Let that be the worse calamity you will face in your bridge journey.

SCORING A SAMPLE RUBBER

We conclude this chapter on scoring by "playing a rubber" in which the WE side wins the Rubber 2-1. We also provide a Rubber Score Card at the end of this Chapter that tallies every Deal, above and below the line. This is a Contract Social Bridge session played in a Rubber Scoring Format which took 10 deals for the two sides to record 3 games between them and identify the winner of the Rubber.

DEAL # 1

WE's final bid is 2-Clubs, requiring 8 tricks in a part-score contract, undoubled. Since this is the first Deal of the Rubber, both sides are non-vulnerable. WE "bid 2 and made 2," "Bridge-Speak" for bidding and making 2 tricks *over* "book." The scoring is as follows: the TSPs for bidding and making 2 minor suit tricks is 20TSPs for each trick. WE side records 40TSPs below the line (BTL), a part-score. At the end of each deal, beginner should review the Score Card in Figure #3. Since this is Deal #1, the 40 TSPs are recorded BTL on the WE side as 40(1) with the (1) signifying that the 40 TSPs came from Deal # 1. BTL TSPs will be "wiped out" for game-counting purposes if THEY makes game before WE; however, for total trick-score purposes, they remain cumulative. The sides' <u>cumulative</u> TSPs are shown below as "Total TSPs," with a side's vulnerability status indicated as "NV" or "V". The Rubber Score line indicates the number of games won by each side in the rubber.

Summary:	WE		THEY	
	TSPs ATL:	0	TSPs ATL	0
	TSPs BTL:	40	TSPs BTL	0
	TOTAL TSPs:	40 NV	TOTAL TSPs:	0 NV
	RUBBER SCORE:	0	RUBBER SCORE:	0

DEAL # 2

THEY's final bid is 3-Hearts, a part-score contract, requiring 9 tricks; the contract is *doubled (for penalty)*. THEY "bid 3 and make 1" resulting in the 2 Undertricks. The trick-score impact of being 2 tricks short, doubled and non-vulnerable is 300TSPs *awarded to THEY, the defense* (100 for the first penalty point and 200 for the second) scored ATL. The score card on the WE side looks like this: 300(2). Since neither side has made game, both are non-vulnerable.

Summary:	WE		THEY	
	TSPs ATL	300	TSPs ATL	
	TSPs BTL	40	TSPs BTL	0
	TOTAL TSPs:	340 NV	TOTAL TSPs:	0 NV
	RUBBER SCORE:	0	RUBBER SCORE	0

DEAL # 3

THEY's final bid is 1-NT, a part-score-contract, undoubled, requiring 7 tricks. THEY "bid 1and made 3," resulting in 2 Overtricks. The trick-score impact of making 1 trick over book in Notrump, undoubled is 40TSPs, for the first trick in Notrump; and, for the 2 Overtricks in Notrump, undoubled *is*, 60 TSPs. Additionally, THEY earn an Honors Bonus of 150 TSPs because one partner held 4 Aces in a Notrump bid. The score card looks like this on the THEY side: 40(3) BTL; and, 210(3) ATL (note the ATL TSPs for the Honors Bonus and Overtricks can be combined for ease of scoring).

Summary:
	WE			THEY	
	TSPs ATL	300		TSPs ATL	210
	TSPs BTL	40		TSPs BTL	40
	TOTAL TSPs:	340 NV		TOTAL TSPs:	250 NV
	RUBBER SCORE: 0			RUBBER SCORE: 0	

DEAL # 4

The WE side's final bid is 6-notrump, a Small Slam, Non-Vulnerable and undoubled. WE "bids 6 and makes 6." The scoring impact of making 6 tricks over book, in Notrump, Non-Vulnerable, undoubled is as follows: 190 TSPs (40 for the first Notrump trick and 150 for the next 5); and, for bidding and making the Small Slam contract while non-vulnerable is a Slam Bonus of 500TSPs. The score card looks like this on the WE side: 190(4) BTL; and 500(4) ATL.

WE's cumulative score BTL is 230TSPs (40, from Deals # 1-3 and 190 from this deal) more than enough for making their first game of the Rubber, for which no points are scored. The Score Sheet protocol when a game is made is to draw a horizontal line through both sides indicating that a game is won. The 230 TSPs remain on the Score Sheet for final settlement purposes. WE, now vulnerable, must cautiously consider, for the remainder of this Rubber, the increased penalties and rewards that may occur. The cumulative score for both sides is shown below under "Total TSPs" as well as WE's first game of the Rubber:

Summary:
	WE			THEY	
	TSPs ATL	800		TSPs ATL	210
	TSPs BTL	230		TSPs BTL	40
	TOTAL TSPs:	1030 V		TOTAL:	250 NV
	RUBBER SCORE: 1			RUBBER SCORE: 0	

DEAL # 5

THEY's final bid, 2-Diamonds is a part-score contract, doubled. THEY "bid 2 and make 4,"resulting in 2 Overtricks. The trick-score impact is as follows: 80TSPs for 2 minor suit tricks made over book doubled; 200 TSPs, (100 for each of the 2 Overtricks), doubled; and 50 TSPs for the "Insult," making a doubled contract. The Score Card on the THEY side looks like this: 80(5) BTL and 250(5) ATL. THEY still are short of game since the 40 TSPs BTL recorded in Deal #3 were "wiped out" when WE made their first game of the Rubber in Deal #4. At this point, THEY have 80 TSPs BTL that will count for making game. The cumulative score for both sides is shown below:

Summary:	WE		THEY	
	TSPs ATL	800	TSPs ATL	460
	TSPs BTL	230	TSPs BTL	120
	TOTAL:	1030 V	TOTAL:	580 NV
	RUBBER SCORE: 1		RUBBER SCORE: 0	

DEAL # 6

WE, Vulnerable, makes a final bid in 4-hearts; a game contract, doubled, Non-Vulnerable. WE "bids 4 and makes 2," going down 2, resulting in 2 Undertricks. The trick-score impact of 2 Undertricks, doubled and vulnerable is as follows: 500 TSPs awarded to the defense. The Score Card on the THEY side looks like this: 500(6) ATL, (200 for the first Undertrick and 300 for the second trick.) As the WE side learns, the failure to fulfill their contract when vulnerable and doubled is expensive. The cumulative totals are shown below:

Summary:	WE		THEY	
	TSPs ATL	800	TSPs ATL	960
	TSPs BTL	230	TSPs BTL	120
	TOTAL TSPs: 1030 V		TOTAL TSPs: 1080 NV	
	RUBBER SCORE: 1		RUBBER SCORE: 0	

DEAL # 7

THEY's final bid is 7-Diamonds, a Grand Slam contract, undoubled and Non-Vulnerable. THEY "bids 7 and makes 7," resulting in a Grand Slam Bonus. The trick-score impact is as follows: 140TSPs for the 7 tricks above book in a minor suit bid and made; and, 1000 TSPs for the Grand Slam bid-and-made when Non-vulnerable. The Score Card on the THEY side looks like this: 140(7) BTL; and, 1000(7) ATL. THEY also win their first game of the Rubber and are now tied with WE in games. The scorer draws the required double line below the score for Trick #7. Also, WE and THEY are now both vulnerable with THEY significantly ahead in Total Score Points.

Summary:	WE		THEY	
	TSPs ATL	800	TSPs ATL	1960
	TSPs BTL	230	TSPS BTL	260
	TOTAL TSPs: 1030 V		TOTAL TSPs: 2220 V	
	RUBBER SCORE: 1		RUBBER SCORE: 1	

DEAL # 8

THEY, Vulnerable, bids 3-NT, a game contract, *doubled*. THEY makes 2," going down 1, resulting in 1 Undertrick. The trick-score impact is 200 TSPs for the 1 Undertrick, doubled and Vulnerable. The score sheet on the WE side looks like this: 200(8) ATL.

Summary:	WE		THEY.	
	TSPs ATL	1000	TSPs ATL	1960
	TSPs BTL	230	TSPs BTL	260
	TOTAL TSPs:	1230 V	TOTAL TSPs:	2220 V
	RUBBER SCORE: 1		RUBBER SCORE: 1	

DEAL # 9

WE, Vulnerable, bids 1-NT, a part-score contract, *doubled*. WE "bids 1 and makes 1," resulting in 1 trick over book, doubled. The trick-score impact is as follows: 80TSPs for the 1TSP in Notrump, doubled. There is also the Insult Bonus of 50T SPs for making a doubled contract. The score sheet on the WE side looks like this: 80(9) BTL, 50(9) ATL.

Summary:	WE		THEY	
	TSPs ATL	1050	TSPs ATL	1960
	TSPs BTL	310	TSPs BTL	260
	TOTAL TSPs:	1360 V	TOTAL TSPs:	2220 V
	RUBBER SCORE: 1		RUBBER SCORE: 1	

DEAL # 10

WE, Vulnerable, bids 6-clubs, a Small Slam, *undoubled*. WE "bids 6 and makes 7," resulting in 1 Overtrick and a Small Slam Bonus. The trick-score impact is as follows: 120TSPs BTL for the 6 minor tricks over book; the Small Slam bonus of 750 TSPs Vulnerable; the 500 TSPs for winning the rubber 2-1 and, the 20 TSPs for the 1 Overtrick Vulnerable. The Score Card on the WE side looks like this: 120(10) BTL; and, 1270(10) ATL.

Summary:	WE		THEY	
	TSPs ATL	2320	TSPS ATL	1960
	TSPs BTL	430	TSPs BTL	260
	TOTAL	2750	TOTAL TSPs:	2220 V
	RUBBER SCORE: 2		RUBBER SCORE: 1	

THE FINAL SETTLEMENT

While the WE side won the Rubber, 2-1, the real prize is the **TOTAL POINT-SCORE,** which was also won by WE by 530 TSPs. At a penny-a-point, each WE partner wins the grand total of $2.65 and bragging rights.

At this point, beginner might be concerned with the amount of memorization required in Scoring. Actually, nothing could be further from the truth! The Scoring Matrix is readily available in many formats and any player can review it at the bridge table *while recording scores on the Score Card (Just like you would do in an open book exam)*. The only retention skills needed are for identifying the Scoring Events, listed above. Understandably, the number of deals required in the Sample to win a Rubber may seem unreasonably high. Actually, they were made artificially long in order to include all the "**SCORING EVENTS**," events which trigger a score that you can expect to encounter. The scenario also added an unrealistic number of Penalty Doubles to emphasize their power when it is successful and pain when it fails. Finally, even though there is no Slam Bidding in beginning bridge, the beginner should understand the scoring impact of a Slam when the other side bids a Slam.

CHAPTER 11
FIGURE # 3

SCORE CARD FOR SAMPLE 10 DEAL RUBBER

	WE	THEY
		1000 (7)
	1270 (10)	500 (6)
	50 (9)	
	200 (8)	250 (5)
	500 (4)	210 (3)
	300 (2)	
===
	40 (1)	40 (3)
	190 (4)	
		80 (5)
		140 (7)
	80 (9)	
	120 (10)	
TOTALS	2750	2220

Footnotes:

- Score Cards can be produced locally simply by horizontally folding in the middle of the sheet for recording scores ATL and BTL. For recording scores for each side fold the sheet vertically in half and title the left half WE and the right half THEY.

- Each trick is identified by a deal #.

- Note that a deal can only belong in one of the two sides.

- When trick-score points involved in a trick are derived from more than one source, they can be combined, but only if they are all ATL or BTL.

CHAPTER 11
FIGURE # 4
SCORING IN DUPLICATE

At this point as you approach the Intermediate Level of bridge, you will find that the bridge game of choice, at that skill level and above is Duplicate Contract Bridge. You will also find it increasingly difficult to turn down invitations to play Duplicate, which uses the Duplicate Scoring Format. While the bidding and the play in Duplicate and Contract is basically the same, the difference in Scoring Formats is significant enough to represent a challenge. For that reason, this section is included in Beginning Bridge to ease your inevitable transition into the world of Duplicate.

In the Duplicate Scoring Format there is no carryover of points from one Deal to the next; a deal is played by two partnerships, known as **PAIRS,** at a numbered table; while at the same time, the exact same deal is bid and played by different Pairs at other numbered tables, with the same vulnerabilities and the same doubled or undoubled contracts. Most importantly, success at duplicate is not dependent on the luck of the deal; rather, success is based on the relative scores made by a number of different Pairs who hold identical cards with identical contracts and identical vulnerabilities. In essence, Duplicate bridge puts Lady Luck almost totally in the closet..

Scoring Events that award points to pairs are essentially, but not exactly the same in both scoring formats. For example, in Duplicate the following **PREMIUM SCORES** apply:

Making game contract is 500 when vul and 300 when nonvul

Bidding and making any part-score contract, nonvul or vul is 50

Bidding and making any doubled contract, nonvul or vul is 50

Bidding and making a Small Slam is 500 nonvul and 750 vul

Bidding and making a Grand Slam is 1000 nonvul and 1500 vul

For each overtrick, trick made in excess of the contract:

Undbl and Nonvul: trick value: Undbl and Vul: trick value
Dbl and Nonvul: 100 and 200 Dbl and vul

For each Undertrick by which declarer falls short of contract:

	Nonvul		Vul	
	Undbl	Dbl	Undbl	Dbl
For 1st Undertrick	50	100	100	200
For ea. additional Undertrick	50	200	100	300

DUPLICATE SCORING TABLE (ABBREVIATED)

The ACBL provides Duplicate Scoring Tables with Total Point-Scores for every possible fulfilled "Bid and Made" Scoring Event from Levels 1-7; whether the side is vul or nonvul; and, the contract dbl or undbl. Each of the 81 "Bid and Made" lines of the Table consists of 6 columns, one of which is shown below for illustrative purposes.

Fulfilled Contracts

Bid	Made	Nonvul		Vul	
		Undbl	Dbl	Undbl	Dbl
3-NT	3	400	550	600	750

Translation: The sample line titled "Bid 3-NT Made 3" is "Bridge-Speak" for 3 tricks over book, bid-and-made in Notrump with **400** points scored under the Nonvul Undbl column. The score is derived as follows: 300 for bidding and making game; and, 100 for the 3 tricks over Book: Trick #7: 40 and 30 each for Tricks #8 and #9 for a total of **400**. Note that the Nonvul Dbl column scores the same Bid 3-NT made 3 as **550** derived as follows: 300 for making game; 200 for the 3 tricks over book (100 doubled); and, 50 for the insult. If the side was Vul the score would be **600** undbl and **750** dbl which also include 50 for the Insult.

Since there are 81 "Bid and Made" Scoring Events for **Fulfilled Contracts** and 13 lines for **Defeated Contracts**, it would be laborious to mentally derive the correct scores in an actual Duplicate environment while Duplicate Boards are being transferred and Pairs are moving between tables. So, don't leave home for your weekly Duplicate game without your ACBL Scoring Table. For information on how to acquire a supply of Tables, contact your nearest bridge club or the ACBL

CHAPTER 12

THE CLIMAX: THE END OF BEGINNING BRIDGE AND THE BEGINNING OF INTERMEDIATE

HOW DO WE KNOW WHEN WE ARE NO LONGER BEGINNERS? THE ANSWER

Remember that question? Well, now you know the answer: all the bridge skills covered in the preceding chapters represent the body of knowledge that a bridge beginner should reasonably be expected to have. Since you have diligently done so, you have reached the end of *Beginning Bridge*. But by no means is that the end of your bridge journey; you are now at the beginning of Intermediate Bridge. The magic of bridge is such that the challenges never end because the varieties of possible deals and the strategies to react to those deals are endless.

At this point, you should begin to cast a wider net for bridge partners: some will not be as up-to-date as you; some will be at the same level; and some will be more advanced. Whatever their level of bridge skill, you will find there is always an opportunity for you to learn more while sharpening your existing skills. When you associate with more advanced players they are very likely to employ some techniques that will be new to you. Don't let that bother you! Ask questions and explore the bridge literature for answers. The big challenge when playing socially with new partners is your ability to articulate a Bidding Agreement Discussion that reflects your skill levels and adapts to the skill level of your new partner.

So, where does the former Beginner go from here? Most likely, if you have come this far, you will want to take the plunge into Intermediate Bridge. Let's look at some of the new skills you will be acquiring.

BRIDGE LIFE BEYOND BEGINNING BRIDGE

While this is far from an all-inclusive list, nor is it in priority order, these are some of the skills you will want to add to your bridge repertoire as soon as possible:

- **CONVENTION CARDS:** In Contract Social Bridge, established partnerships develop an informal bidding agreement between themselves, not reduced to a formal written agreement. Its main purpose is to facilitate the bidding conversation and ensure that what is bid is in the hand of the bidder. Once you start playing with strangers, you are likely in a much more structured environment than party bridge; and, as a result it is important that you have a process by which you can uniformly describe to your opponents what system, conventions, methods of leads, discards and signals your are using. The vehicle used to transmit this information to opponents is the **CONVENTION CARD**; a preprinted form listing commonly used conventions so that players simply have to place checkmarks. Open spaces are provided so that players can write in conventions or understandings not in the printed card. Convention Cards also have a section for providing guidance on selecting opening lead cards based on whether the play is versus a suit or versus Notrump. In the end, there are no secrets between opponents and skillful use of the Convention Card is the method for ensuring that there are no misunderstandings regarding the methods used for selecting opening lead cards.

- **DUPLICATE CONTRACT BRIDGE:** Your new Intermediate level bridge friends more than likely prefer Duplicate over Contract Social Bridge because it eliminates the luck of the deal. In Duplicate, your side's Vulnerability and your contract's Doubled or Undoubled status is predetermined by the numbered Duplicate Scoreboard and the Table assigned to your partnership; and, since the same deal is played by more than one pair of players luck is not involved in the outcome, only the score made by your partnership compared to what the other pairs made. From many aspects Duplicate is similar to Contract: there is an Auction; guidelines for Openings, Opening Leads, Overcalling, Responding, Advancing and the Play of the Tricks are basically the same. This is an excellent venue for recent beginners to meet their next bridge challenge. As discussed in Chapter 11 the biggest difference between the two formats is the Scoring. Perhaps the best feature of Duplicate is that Lady Luck remains in the closet.

- **THE COMPETITIVE AUCTION** usually refers to bidding sequences in which both sides enter the auction. Within the context of this discussion, we are referring to auctions that require a number of bidding rounds with both sides competing to arrive at their side's best contract. In *Beginning Bridge*, we usually ended the Auction after the first or second Rounds, with little or no competition from the other side. In more competitive Auctions, the bidding continues well beyond that, with all players getting at least another chance to bid again, a **REBID**. The skills needed to compete at that level require guidance for making rebids by openers and responders. Bidding is a conversation that should not stop until you and your partner have the best possible understanding of what is in each others' hands. More importantly, skill in bidding insures that your side will not miss the opportunity to make the best fit between your final contract and the holdings in your combined hand. Specific skills in competitive auctions include the Third Seat's options after the Second Seat Overcalls or Doubles for Takeout; the Fourth Seat's options when the Second Seat bids; and, Opener's reaction when his LHO Overcalls and his partner in the Third Seat advances with a Double (the Negative Double) or a Cuebid which is only available in a competitive auction; and, when you are the First Seat, Second Seat Overcalls and your partner in the Third Seat Cuebids.

- **SLAM BIDDING:** A Slam is the brass ring of bridge; do not foreclose your chance at grabbing it as you transition beyond beginning bridge. Slam bidding involves such conventions as the Blackwood and Gerber which identify the availability of Aces and Kings respectively before making a final slam bid. *Beginning Bridge* caps the bidding at the 3-5 levels in Notrump, major suit or minor suit bidding, respectively because there is no scoring advantage to bid beyond those levels without Slam Bidding skills. However, in Intermediate Bridge, you have reached the point where you cannot afford to not know what to do when you and your partner have a shot at making a Slam. Successful Slams earn huge bonuses. While Slams are relatively rare, they occur frequently enough that you will greatly disappoint partner if you cannot rise to the occasion.

- **TWO-OVER-ONE GAME FORCE:** A bidding method based on the convention that responder's 2-level response in a lower ranking suit to opener's 1-level bid suit is forcing to game. For example, 1-heart---pass---2-clubs; or, 1-spade---pass---2-diamonds. This system is very widely used and, as you start to travel in different circles, you will be asked if you play it. The basis for this method is that it allows partners, in conjunction with the Five Card Majors system, to test slam possibilities while the bidding is still low. It is not a new bidding system since it can be incorporated into your current bidding system. It is particularly effective for exploring Slam possibilities.

- **DOUBLE FOR PENALTY:** In beginning bridge you have learned what this Double means within the context of scoring. However, what was not discussed was how to determine *when* you should Double for Penalty; including when it is likely that you will or will not succeed. Also not discussed was the strategy for dealing with a Double immediately following a Notrump Opening bid. In the end, the Double for Penalty, when used properly is a formidable weapon. As discussed, if the Advancer does not "takeout" partner's Takeout Double by advancing, the double is a "ticking time bomb that could become "for penalty."

- **SIGNALING:** is the language used by defenders for legally exchanging information about their holdings. It is done when following to a suit or when discarding. While there are a large number of different methods, the most common is the "attitude signal" which communicates information about their hands by playing specific cards. For example, if a defender wants his partner to continue leading a suit a suit, the signal could be to play the highest card available; and, if partner want to discourage the playing of a suit, the signal could be to play the lowest card available. Signaling should be a part of the intermediate players' bidding agreement.

- **BALANCING:** If first seat opens and next two seats pass, the fourth seat is in the **PASSOUT SEAT** since a pass would be the third consecutive pass resulting in a new auction. Balancing is the term used to describe a player's position wherein, if he passes, the auction ends. If the fourth seat's partner, with a fairly good hand, passed because he had no way to describe his hand within the confines of the bidding agreement, the Fourth Seat's pass may result in the side walking away from a positive scoring opportunity. On the other hand, if the fourth seat Balances, enters the bidding with less than opening strength, also known as one with **SLENDER VALUES,** the side has an opportunity to compete. There is a considerable amount of bridge literature that discusses this dilemma: to balance or to pass, much of which is considered beyond *Beginning Bridge*.

- **REDOUBLE:** A call that that follows an opposing double for penalty. It doubles all scores: penalties, trick-scores and overtrick premiums. Game or slam contracts may attract redoubles. Redoubled contracts are rare in beginning bridge play and like Slam Bidding the Redouble was not included in beginning bridge since it is encountered when the standard of play is high. It is now time to become familiar with it.

SOURCES FOR SKILLS BEYOND BEGINNING BRIDGE

While there is no shortage of reference books for intermediate and advanced bridge, the *Official Encyclopedia of Bridge* is the most comprehensive source of bridge information for all levels of bridge players, but especially for intermediate and advanced beginners. The *Bridge Player's Dictionary is an excellent alternative to the OEB*. As needed, *individual lessons* with qualified bridge teachers are the best approach since they are the most efficient way to focus on your specific bridge deficiencies. An excellent book for the beginning intermediate player is William S. Root's *How to Play a Bridge Hand.* The book's flap readily admits that "…This book is not for experts, nor for beginners, but it is for the 90% of the players in between." That description fits you, the newly-minted intermediate player! Finally, since bridge is constantly evolving, it is important to keep current; and, the best way to do that is to join the American Contract Bridge League (800-467-1623) and receive their monthly bulletin. In each issue, there is an excellent section in the bulletin devoted to your skill level.

FINIS

Hopefully, you end with a resolve to continue on with your bridge journey. Now, go find that bridge partner and start that conversation!

BIBLIOGRAPHY

Arnold, Peter: *Basic Bridge: Octopus Publishing Group, 2003*

Brown, Randal: *The Bridge Players' Dictionary:* Devyn Press, 1993

Francis, Henry: *Official Encyclopedia of Bridge, Sixth Edition,* ACBL, 2001

Grant, Audrey: *Bridge Basics 1, Bridge Basics 2*: Baron Barclay, 2005

Manley, Brent: *The Tao of Bridge:* Adams Media, 2005

Pavlicek, Richard: *Bridge Writing Style Guide*: Internet Download (www.rebridge.net7z69), 2000

Richardson, Brian, *Introduction to the Science of Bidding,* Xlibris, 2006

Root, William: *How to Play A Bridge Hand*: Crown Publishers.1990

GLOSSARY OF BRIDGE TERMS/INDEX

ABOVE-THE-LINE (ATL): Bonus Points on Rubber Score card not scored towards game (page 125, 139)

ADVANCE: Fourth Seat's response to partner's Overcall or Takeout Double (page 27, 75)

ALERT: Partner's Oral announcement, ensuring opponents' awareness that bid is Conventional (page 40, 57)

ARTIFICIAL OPENING: Opening bid with a Conventional meaning does not denote a holding (page 30)

AUCTION: Bidding Process which decides on the final Contract, (page 15, 39)

BALANCED HANDS: 3 shapes defined numerically as follows: 5-3-3-2, 4-3-3-3, 4-4-3-2 (page 17, 53)

BALANCING BID: When Fourth Seat, after two consecutive passes, opens with "slender values" (page 81, 139)

BEGINNER'S BIDDING LADDER: shows tricks required at each of the 35 bidding levels (page 20, 23)

BELOW-THE-LINE (BTL): Trick-Score Point on Rubber Score Card counting towards game page 127, 133)

BEST MINOR: When 5-card major or Notrump openings not available, best minor suit is selected (page 29)

BID: Includes one of the five strains and one of the 7 bidding levels; a Double is also a bid (page 15)

BIDDING AGREEMENT DISCUSSION: Script for new partners, indicating Conventions used (page 16, 41)

BIDDING CONVERSATION: Record of Auction's, limited in number of words than can be used (page 103)

BIDDING DIAGRAM: Illustrates the entire Auction from start to the last pass (page 18)

BIDDING ROUND: When all four player have made a call (Bid, Pass or Double) (page 40)

BIDDING SEQUENCE: Series of bidding rounds, starting from the first round to the last (page 40)

BIDDING SPACE: Bidding room provided to partner to facilitate his response in an Auction, (page 27)

BIDDING SYSTEM---sum of partnership's understandings that make up their language of bidding (27)

BIDDING UP-THE-LINE: Bidding protocol for ascending in suit rank order: i.e. Hearts, then Spades (page 58)

BLACKWOOD: Advanced bid usually in 4-notrump, asking for Aces; seeking First Round Control (page 138)

BOOK: The first six tricks made in the play, only tricks made above book earn Trick-Score Points (page 94)

BROKEN SEQUENCE: Sequence of 3 Honor cards with one of middle cards missing: for example, AQJ (page 88)

BROKEN SUIT: A suit which contains no cards adjacent in rank: for example, 10753 (page 88)

CALL: Any Bid, Double or Pass made in an Auction (page 27)

CARD DIAGRAM: Illustrates the hands held by one to four players (page 17)

CARDING DECISION: Choosing card in suit selected for an Opening Lead; shown in Convention Card (page 86)

CHEAPEST LEVEL AVAILABLE: Lowest bid that is both legal and not higher than necessary (page 43)

COMBINED HAND: The 26 cards in the hands of the two partners (page 19)

COMMUNICATION PROBLEM: The challenge to transfer lead from one hand to another (page 93)

COMPETITIVE AUCTION: Bidding Sequences when both sides enter the Auction (page 39, 138)

CONTRACT: Promise by Auction's winners to make a specific number of tricks in strain selected (page 39)

CONTRACT DOUBLED FOR PENALTY: When one side believes final bid will not make (page 12, 125)

CONVENTIONAL BID:--Bid with defined meaning known by partner, not a Natural Bid, not a secret (page 31)

CONVENTION CARD: List of Conventions, Leads, Systems, Signals, used in formal settings (page 90, 143)

COUNTING: Mental tracking of High Cards played, especially when drawing trumps (page 95)

CUEBID: Conventional bid, in opening suit bid, with no intention of using it; forcing; shows strength (page 76)

DATA POINT EVENTS: Information required by Declarer to make the Plan of the Play (page 100)

DECLARER: First player to mention strain in which Contract is played, controls play of combined hand (page 19)

DECLARER'S ANALYSIS: Analysis necessary for formulating the Plan of the Play (page 103)

DECLARER PLAY: Play in which Declarer controls dummy and own hand; starts after opening lead (page 20, 93)

DEFINE THE CONTRACT: In terms of the strain selected and the number of tricks required (page 15, 39)

DEFICIT: When Tally of Sure Winners is less than the Winners required by the contract (page 94)

DELAYED WINNERS: Cards that become Winners after the first or second time its suit is led (page 20, 96)

DEVELOPING TRICKS: Using options that create extra needed tricks, skills available to the beginner (page 96)

DISCARD: A card played to a trick not of the suit led and is not trump (18, 97)

DISTRIBUTION: The cards held in each suit within a hand; a. k. a. Shape (page 17)

DIVIDE: Probabilities of the ways in which suit lengths can be fractionated (page 67)

DOUBLED FOR PENALTY: A bid by defense to doubly penalize declarers if contract is set (page 33, 80, 139)

DOUBLE FOR TAKEOUT: Bid, with opening strength, asks partner to select one unbid suit as trump, (page 46)

DRAWING TRUMPS: Bridge Event that renders the enemy void of their trumps (page 94)

DUCKING A TRICK: Declining to take a trick that one likely could have won (107, 121)

DUMMY POINTS: Shortness Points assigned to dummy in lieu Length Points after fit identified (page 19)

DUPLICATE" Pairs playing same deal as at other tables, standings determined by comparisons (page 12,134,138)

END-GAME: The final bridge events that include the Plan of the Play and the Play of the Tricks (page 93)

ESTABLISHED: Partnership that has often played together (page 40)

FINESSE: Developing an extra trick by trapping an opponent's High Card, 50% success rate (page 98)

FIRST ROUND CONTROL: With Aces, side can prevent Opening Leader from taking first trick (page 31)

FIT: When responder has 3-card or more support for Opening suit bid; results in an 8-card or more fit (page 51)

FIVE-CARD MAJORS, BEST MINOR: A bidding system opening with a 5-card major or best minor (page 29)

FORCING: A Bid that requires partner to respond (page 30, 33)

FULFILLED: When a side makes all the tricks its contract promised (page 139)

FULL DEAL: In a Card Diagram when all 4 Hands are displayed with 13 cards in each Hand (page 18)

GAME BID: A bid with just enough tricks to make game in the selected strain (page 61)

GAME GOING BID: Responder with enough strength to insist on game (page 61)

GERBER: Advanced convention used in Slam Bidding to identify Aces, 4-Clubs after 1-NT: (page 138)

GO DOWN: To be short in the required number of tricks promised, results in Undertricks (page 15)

GOLDEN FIT:A fit of at least 8-trump cards in the Declarers' combined hand (page 53,54)

GOOD SUIT: A suit with two of the top three or three of the top five Honor Cards (page 23)

GRAND SLAM, A contract requiring 13 tricks that must be bid-and-made in order to earn a Bonus (page 20)

GUARDS: Spot cards that back up the High Card Stopper (page28)

GUARDED SUIT: A suit headed by any High Card, prevents a run when play is in Notrump (page 28)

GUIDELINES: Suggestions, such as minimum bidding levels, not Laws, evolving over time, (page 15)

HAND: The 13 cards held by any one of the four players, a.k.a known as Holdings (page 16)

HAND VALUATION: Estimation of a hand's trick-taking potential, using a Point-Count System (page 19)

HIGH CARDS: Face Cards, AKQJ, enables players to make hand valuations (page 16)

HIGH CARD POINTS: Points derived from High Cards, AKQJ are 4,3,2,1 points respectively (page 19)

HONORS BONUS POINTS: Bonus Points for special holdings, such as all 4 Aces when in Notrump (page 124)

HONOR CARDS: AKQJ10, the top five cards (page 16)

IMPERFECT FIT: 7-card fit, yields disproportionately less tricks than an 8-card Golden Fit (page 53, 54)

INITIAL POINT-COUNT: Derived only from High Cards and Length (page 19)

INSULT BONUS: Bonus score of 50 points for making a doubled contract (page 124)

INTERFERENCE: A Double or Overcall that interferes in a non-competitive Auction, see Obstruction (page 44)

INVITATIONAL HAND: Responder, with extra values encourages opener to continue bidding (page 59)

JACOBY: See Transfer Bid (page 57)

JUMP OVERCALL: Overcall made one or more levels higher than necessary (page 44)

JUMP SHIFT: a jump in a new suit by responding hand, normally forcing to game (page 63)

LAW 41 OF CONTRACT BRIDGE: The Bidding Process' "Bill of Rights" (page 40)

LAWS OF CONTRACT BRIDGE: Unlike guidelines, when Laws are broken, penalties will be applied (page 15)

LAW OF TOTAL TRICKS: Theory that total trumps in combined hand equals a safe bidding level (page 54)

LENGTH: Develops tricks by leading long suits until defenders are void in that suit (page 17, 97)

LENGTH POINTS: Points added for 5-card or longer suits (page 19)

LIGHT: Bid with strength slightly below range suggested by guidance, usually when balancing (page 78)

LIMIT BID: Bid that places a limit on the Hand's strength, reduces need for describing hand's strength (page 28)

LONG SUIT: With 4-Cards or more a suit has length and is also known as LONG (page 17, 26)

MADE: Deck that is properly shuffled and cut or a contract successfully fulfilled (page 16)

MAKE: To fulfill a contract, as in, "the contract makes." (page112)

MAXIMUM OPENING STRENGTH: for a 1-level opening bid: 19-21VPs (page 35)

MAXIMUM OVERCALL: Overcall made with opening strength, 13-17VPs and good 5-card suit (page 76)

MEDIUM OPENING STRENGTH: 17-18VPs (page 35)

MINIMUM OPENING STRENGTH: opening bid with as little as 13-16VPs (page 35)

MINIMUM OVERCALL: Overcall made with less than opening 7-12HCPs and good 5-card suit (page76)

MISDEAL: When player is dealt more or less than 13 cards, or with card faced-up, Dealer re-deals (page 16)

NATURAL BID: Call that reflects the character of the hand, no artificial meaning (page 30)

NEGATIVE DOUBLE: AKA Responder's Double, asks opener to select trump suit from unbid suits (page 66)

NEW SUIT: An unbid suit in the Auction, usually forcing (page 27, 73)

ON-THE-BOARD: In Declarer Play when next trick is from the dummy (page 95)

OPENING BID: The first bid in an auction (page 15)

OPENING LEAD: First card in the play, made by the defense before dummy becomes visible (page 87)

OPENING LEADER: Declarer's LHO, always makes the opening lead (page 25)

OPENING STRENGTH: At least 13VPs, the minimum needed to open the bidding in a suit (page 30)

OVERCALL: A Call made by the opener's LHO, promises good 5-card suit and 7-17VPs (page 43)

OVERTRICKS: Tricks made in excess of the contract, do not count towards game; (page 124)

PAIRS: Term used in Duplicate to describe numbered partnerships (page 134)

PART-SCORE: Contract for tricks less than the minimum needed to make game (page 30, 126)

PASS-OUT SEAT: Seat in which third pass results in the end of the auction (145)

PENALTY POINTS: Points for defense for each Undertrick, tricks which falls short of the contract (page 15, 31)

PERFECT BRIDGE HAND: can make 13 tricks, if played in Notrump; or, 13 cards in 1-suit if played in that suit (page 20, 66)

PLAN OF THE PLAY: Declarer's plan for fulfilling the contract, making overtricks and minimizing penalties (page 93)

PLAY OF THE TRICKS: AKA "The Play;" 13 tricks are played to determine if contract is fulfilled (page 15, 93)

PLAYING-TRICKS: Tricks in a single hand that can be won after a Sacrifice Play if any, is made (page 21)

POINT-COUNT SYSTEMS: Valuation methods, numerical values to determine hand's trick-taking potential (page 19)

POSITIVE RESPONSE: Reply to 2-Club Strong Opening, other than Artificial 2-Diamond Waiting bid (page 65)

PREEMPTIVE OPENING BID: Made with a weak hand and a Good 6-card, 7-card or 8-card suit (page 31)

PREEMPTIVE OVERCALL: Weak, one or more levels higher than necessary, consumes space (page 42, 75)

PROMOTION: By driving out other side's higher ranking cards, remaining cards promoted to winners (page 97)

RAISE:--Response increasing the bidding level last made by partner (page 61)

REBID: Player's second bid (page 138)

REDEAL: A second deal required after a misdeal, keeps the same dealer (page 17)

RESPONDER: Player whose priority is to provide Support for the Opening bid or Double (page 19, 53)

RESPONDER'S DOUBLE: AKA Negative Double, asking partner to select an unbid suit (page 66)

RUBBER: A game match in which first side to win 2 games scores a Rubber Bonus (page 15, 123)

RUBBER BONUS: Premium points awarded to the first side that wins 2 games (page 15, 123)

RUBBER BRIDGE: Synonymous with Contract Social Bridge and Rubber Scoring Format (page 123)

RUBBER SCORE CARD: Defined form on which scores entered for each deal in Contract Bridge (page 133)

RUFF: Play a trump on the lead of a Side Suit in which you are void (page 26)

RULE OF 11: If 4th highest card of a suit led is a 7, number of cards higher than it are 4 (page 88)

RULE OF 20: With only 10 HCPs, if sum of cards in two longest suits total 10, open bidding Naturally (page 30)

RULE OF 2 AND 3: When Sacrificing, do not go down more than 2 if Vulnerable and 3 if Non-Vul (page 31)

RULE OF 15: Open, following 3 passes when HCPs plus sum of Spade cards adds to 15 (page 40)

SACRIFICE PLAY: When a card is played to draw a higher card so remaining cards become winners (page 21, 96)

SACRIFICE BID: Hope that points lost are fewer than opponents would score in their own contract (page 33, 112)

SCORE CARD: Defined form for Scoring in a Rubber Scoring Format (page 133)

SCORING EVENT: An event, such as winning a game, that results in points scored (page 1231)

SEQUENCE: Two or more Honor Cards in same suit in consecutive ranking order (page 88)

SHAPE: Numerical description of number of cards within each of a hand's four suits, example: 5-3-3-2 (page 17)

SHORT SUIT: Any 2-card or less suit; a 3-card suit is neither short nor long (page 17)

SHORTNESS: Describes hand with a void, a singleton or a doubleton; enhances trick-taking potential (page 17, 19)

SIDE SUIT: A suit other than the trump suit (page 95)

SIGNALING: Codes used by the defense when following to a suit and when discarding (page 88, 138)

SIMPLE SUIT OVERCALL: Overcall made at the Cheapest Level available (page 43)

SLAM BIDDING: Advanced skill using Convention to gain first round control in Slam play (page 31, 139)

SLAM BONUS POINTS: Points which must be bid-and-made in order to be earned (page 124)

SPOT CARD: Non-Face Cards ranging from the 10 to 2 inclusive; 10 is also an Honor Card (page 16)

STAYMAN: Artificial 2-Club response to notrump opening seeking a 4—4 card match in a major (page 57)

STOPPERS: High Cards in Notrump declarer's hand that guard against an immediate run of a suit (page 25)

STRAIN: Describes suits and Notrump collectively, AKA known as a denomination (page 16)

STRONG HAND: A single hand's holding of 20 or more points (page 30)

STRONG OPENING BIDS: Openings in 2-Notrump or 2-Club Artificial Strong Opening (page 30, 65)

STRENGTH: A hand's trick-taking potential measured in Valuation Points (page 16)

SUB-MINIMAL OPENING: Less than opening strength used in making an opening bid (page 30)

SUITABLE FOR NOTRUMP: Balanced Hand with 15-17HCPs and at least 3 guarded suits (page 28)

SUIT COMBINATION: The way the cards in a single suit are divided within a side (page 20)

SUPPORT: 3-Cards or more held in Responder in the same suit as the opening suit (page 53)

SURE LOSER: A trick that is certain to be lost if led (page 94)

SURE WINNER: A card that will surely make a trick without losing a lead (page 19, 93)

TAKEOUT DOUBLE: AKA Double for Takeout, not intended for Penalty (page 41)

TALLY: Declarer's count of Sure Winners, taken after the dummy is visible (page 19)

TOTAL POINT-SCORE: Within a Rubber, the sum of all points earned ATL or BTL (page 60, 94 125)

TOUCHING HONORS: Honor Cards in a Sequence (page 88)

TRADE-OFF ANALYSIS:: Determines if cost of losing is less than cost of other side making (page 33, 123)

TRANSFER BID: Artificial, after 1-notrump opening, shows ranking of suit immediately below suit bid (page 56)

TRANSPORTATION PROBLEM---see Communication Problem (page 26, 93)

TRAP PASS: Pass when holding a strong hand in opponent's suit (page 44)

TRICK SCORE POINTS: Points for tricks counting towards game, based on the strain played (page 33, 124)

TRUMPING LOSERS IN DUMMY: Ruffing a Sure Loser with one of the dummy's trumps (page 98)

TRUMP SUIT MANAGEMENT: When Declarer keeps mental track of all his trumps (page 96)

TWO OVER ONE GAME FORCE: 2-level response to opener's 1-level opening forces to game page 138)

TWO DIAMONDS WAITING BID: Artificial response to 2-club opening, opener to describe his hand (page 65)

UNFAVORABLE DIVIDE: When a side splits to a player's disadvantage (page 96)

UNDERBID: To make a bid intentionally or unintentionally with weaker hand than actually held (page 33, 123)

UNDERTRICK: Trick that falls short of the contract (page 33, 123)

VALUATION POINTS: Sum of Length Points and High Card Points in an initial point-count (page 19)

VIRTUAL BRIDGE: Simulated, as opposed to Real Bridge (page 99)

VULNERABLE: A side that has already won a game (page 33, 123)

WEAK-TWO OPENING: 2-level opening with 5-10 and any Good 6-card suit, considered preemptive (page 31)

CPSIA information can be obtained
at www.ICGtesting.com
Printed in the USA
BVHW011919040522
636159BV00012B/235